# ATLANTIS *A NEW VIEW*

**Louise Ingraham**

Bizy Enterprises, Inc. – Publisher – Gilbert, Arizona

# ATLANTIS *A NEW VIEW*

**Author: Louise Ingraham**

Published by:
**Bizy Enterprises, Inc.**
929 N. Val Vista Dr.
Suite 107 #191
Gilbert, Arizona 85234

All rights reserved. No part of this book or illustrations may be reproduced or transmitted in any form or by any means, electronic or mechanical, including photocopying, recording or by any information storage and retrieval system without written permission from Bizy Enterprises, Inc. Copies may be obtained only by direct orders through Bizy Enterprises, Inc.

Grateful acknowledgement is made to Unique for the permission to tell her story.

Copyright 2004
ISBN, first print edition 0-9722621-0-5
Publishing date: May, 2004

Bizy Enterprises, Inc. retains all rights and ownership to **"ATLANTIS *A New View*"** for publishing and distribution.

## CONTENTS

ABOUT THE AUTHOR
ACKNOWLEDGEMENT
INTRODUCTION

| | |
|---|---:|
| CHAPTER I: VISIONS | 1 |
| CHAPTER II: MEMORIES OF ITALY | 17 |
| CHAPTER III: A JOURNEY INTO THE UNKNOWN | 35 |
| CHAPTER IV: FIRST GLIMPSE OF ATLANTIS | 49 |
| CHAPTER V: PRIESTS ON THE MOUNTAIN | 63 |
| CHAPTER VI: RICHA'S PLAN | 77 |
| CHAPTER VII: EVILS OF ATLANTIS | 89 |
| CHAPTER VIII: EVIL VERSUS GOOD | 103 |
| CHAPTER IX: THE POWER TO DESTROY | 115 |
| CHAPTER X: THE EXODUS AND FALL | 127 |
| CHAPTER XI: LIVES AFFECTED BY ATLANTIS | 143 |
| CHAPTER XII: EGYPT AFTER ATLANTIS | 159 |
| CHAPTER XIII: FROM ATLANTIS TO NOW | 175 |

## ABOUT THE AUTHOR

"ATLANTIS *A New View*", was written by Louise Ingraham about an age old mystery that reveals the existence of an island called Atlantis.

She is an author that allows the reader to follow a story as if one is a part of the experience. She challenges the traditional format of writing. Her main character's dialog is written in bold so that the story can easily be followed. Her style of writing is fast moving and exciting but is also filled with intrigue that reveals the unknown.

One can find our author's works in other published books, **"Sapiens Journey Through Time and Space" and "The Pioneer Spirit of Minnie and Charley Williams"**. Both of these books can be ordered from the form in the back of the book.

# ACKNOWLEDGEMENT

I want to thank Unique for her trust in my ability to tell her story. I commend her for the courage it took to release the knowledge that others may view as skeptical.

A loving thank you to my daughter, Mary Ann Hicks for the tedious task of editing, and to my son-in-law Milton Hicks, for getting it ready for publication through their website, "www.mindseyevision.com."

A special thanks to my husband, Willard Ingraham, for his part in editing as well as his patience and support that he gave me during long hours of writing in solitude.

I am grateful to Shannon Hicks and Ryan Peters for their insight into the designs I needed. Ryan's brilliant cover and chapter illustrations are powerful visionaries for new awareness. Posters of these illustrations and other works can be obtained from ordering on the website, "www.mindseyevision.com."

## INTRODUCTION

"ATLANTIS *A New View*" is more than a story of life in another century. It takes the mind to a distant place in time in which many only speculate, existed. The mystery behind Atlantis is revealed through descriptive narrative told by the author's friend, Unique, who believes she holds the secrets of Atlantis in her own memories.

This book was written so that others may share an experience and envision the people of Atlantis. What is written challenges ones own center of reality in an exciting adventure.

Reading a story does not make it true; challenging what one reads opens new doors to new possibilities. This book extends those views for all to see.

As the author, I am humbled that Unique has chosen me to share her story with others. It is her own story told in her own way that implores one to see beyond.

# CHAPTER I:
## VISIONS

To have visions that are credible is a controversial phenomenon at best. The question is; are visions fact or fiction or somewhere in between? Fact, because all of us can recall experiencing visions during our sleep. Fiction, because most of our visions happen when we are in a dream state. The visions I am about to relate came to my view in quite another way.

It happened like this: I was visiting my friend Unique at her home in the city, for a few days. It was a beautiful late summer afternoon when I arrived. There was excitement at seeing my friend and time spent catching up with the family news. After a lovely dinner Unique decided we would sit on her patio in the garden. It was just after dusk when we settled into comfortable lounging chairs. The night air was warm and comfortable with a slight breeze stirring. The moon was in full view but the sky was dark enough that the stars stood out like beacon lights.

I could see the outline of Unique's face from the light reflecting off the moon. It was obvious that her concentration was focused on the skies to the north. As she spoke, it was as if she was one with the stars. I was immobilized by her transfixion.

Unique spoke, **"I can move my mind to see into the past. I have learned to do this with my desire to see beyond. I see visions of my life long ago in another time and degree. I am in this century on earth that we now live, but the visions that I see come before me as if I am a part of a 3D movie. I am there; I am living another time as though it is happening. I see myself; I am that person I see and it is my own life that I am viewing. I feel and** speak and know as if I am actually there. This person, Unique, as you know me, is bodily here, but my mind is full of visions that have taken me beyond.

You have known me for a very long time and we have shared many things. In spite of this sharing I have never had the courage to tell you this part of my life before now. The reality is that I have always been fearful of what others will think.

My fears come from having experienced the rejections I have felt over the years, by talking about my visions. I have been especially hurt by the rejections from my own family members. They said that my visions were dreams and had no reality. I was shamed for telling untruths and called an incurable dreamer. Those memories have left fear in my mind that kept me from talking about any visions that I might have. It was not until I married a man who believed in me that I found I could be comfortable with my disclosure and then only with a few people.

You are wondering why I am telling you that now. The first reason is because you will listen and not be judgmental. I know that you understand that an open mind allows us to use ones own desire to pursue ones own enlightenment.

Secondly, I consider my visions as gifts that are only possible because a higher power has allowed me to experience them. I realize that everyone has gifts from a higher power. One may call this higher power a name that they believe is right as long as a higher power is recognized. I believe that this higher power is God and that it is God's plan that we are to share our gifts with others. In this way we are sharing our gifts for the growth of the soul.

# VISIONS

I have found that over time I have developed very strong spiritual convictions. You know that I believe that freedom of willpower activates the growth of the soul and is one of the greatest spiritual gifts that God has given each of us. It is the growth of the soul that is entwined in our spirituality. It is this spiritual growth that we understand. Our spiritual growth begins with having freewill to make choices. It is our desire that activates our freewill. If our desire is spiritual in nature and actively directed in a way that is for the good of others we are sharing enlightenment. This enlightenment helps others to activate their own freewill with desires to follow their own spiritual path in their own ways. In this way an act of sharing becomes the movement for spiritual growth. I now believe my visions appear from my soul. I believe the visions I see are gifts from God and are meant to be shared.

Although I have strong convictions I am aware that I will receive criticism from those who do not believe my visions are real. I can handle disbelief but it is difficult to accept when my visions are called impossible lies. It has always seemed easier to avoid this kind of criticism by remaining silent. I realize though, to overcome fear, I must face up to it. It is only because of my strong desires to share my gifts for good that gives me the courage to reveal my visions openly to others. In that concept I have turned to you to help me share what I see. I realize that the sharing of my own visions may be the enlightenment that others need to arouse their own desire.

The topic around the visions that I will disclose to you tonight is as controversial as the fact that I can see visions. Especially so, because these visions include past memories of the time that I lived on the island of Atlantis.

# ATLANTIS *A New View*

There is yet another disclosure you must know about my visions before I begin. My mind sees that my present and future is affected by my past. I value what I have learned through my visions of my past because it helps me find the right answers in my present life. When my mind knows the answers from my past I can readily present my findings to use for the benefit of finding the right answers for my present life. In other words, when my mind finds the past and presents these findings so that it may be a part of the present, I have a whole picture to view. Although the past is in other centuries, what happened then becomes parallel to events of today. When I say this I am thinking of the corruption in the time of Atlantis to be parallel to the corruption of today. We learn from past experiences in ways that help us make correct decisions now and we can see the value from knowing the past. This process is no different than looking back at other historical events that help us find the right way to proceed.

I will go one step further into this philosophy. When I speak of my past memories, I speak of a time of my life that existed far from the reaches of what is considered our past during this lifetime on earth. These messages and visions that I gather from other past times I consider as wisdom. Wisdom being the answers from others in another time to help another find answers for the present. It is simple in retrospect. What I find from the past is added to what I know of the present and from this whole spectrum I can make the right decisions in my life today that will carry over into the future."

Unique hesitated and I reassured my friend, "I do know you well and I do believe you have visions if you say you do. I am intrigued by your disclosure of Atlantis. I have always wanted to learn more about this existence and I am grateful you are willing to share your experiences with me."

Unique chuckled as she said, **"You still amaze me after all of the years we have been friends your impatience still shows. I can hear in your voice your excitement when you speak of Atlantis. It makes me comfortable knowing you want me to share but the story of my visions begins long before Atlantis. I have a prelude that needs to be heard and digested into your mind before we open the door into Atlantis."**

I nodded my head in affirmation.

Unique began to reminisce in a quiet audible voice. Her voice was lifted softly to the night skies as she spoke, **"It is in the thought process that my mind finds visions from memories in another time. My memories are kept forever in my soul. There is an inseparable link between my mind and soul. I call these memories from the soul, messages in my mental encyclopedia. I use thoughts to separate those pages and to find those places that hold the answers that I seek. It is the mind that then translates those times into visions and messages for me to understand.**

**As I tell my story I will be taking my mind into the recesses of my soul and into another time. The energy forces around me transport my mind via the thought process into other dimensions. In the beginning, my first visions were as child like as I was. I had no understanding of the thought process and acted as a child reaching out. I had no value of the concept of what I was doing. I believe now, looking back that many of my visions, at that time, in my life did actually come to me as dreams.**

Children are so innocent in their willingness to travel with the mind. It is a natural phenomenon for them to have visions. The mind of a child is so ready to absorb everything around them. It is others that either encourage or dispel what the child sees and hears. It is not to say that in some things a child speaks and it is truly prattle but there are other times they should be taken seriously. It is the adult that must recognize the difference by listening with an open mind before they decide.

In my case I found that no one took me seriously. Many of my first visions were about something that had not yet happened. The visions I recall as the most vivid were the visions where I saw injuries or sickness to a family member and on occasion death. My peers thought that what I said was a vision was actually what I had learned after the fact.

Looking back I can see how this could have happened. I was a child with a great imagination and often placed myself into stories of enchantment that had been read or told to me. It is not unusual for a child to do this. Later as I learned to read on my own I was able to separate fantasy from reality easily. I suppose, as a child, it may have seemed to others that I lived more in a fantasy world.

I know that in disclosing this about myself I am adding possible skepticism as to if I have visions or do I imagine them? In truth, the visions I had as a child were mostly frightening to me. They were especially frightening when I saw someone I cared for in harms way.

Now that I look back, I don't believe the visions I had as a child were meant to frighten me. I believe now that it was God's way in allowing me a vision that would buffer the shock of what was to come. As a child I did not understand this. I have come to believe our visions are a gift and are given to us to see and understand for the purpose of good.

I can recall how I first realized I could direct my thoughts to my soul to find specific information. This was a time of discovery for me; a time I could finally connect the link between my desires and my thoughts. It happened one evening as I was sitting outdoors watching the stars. I must have been in my early teens because it was about that time that we were studying about the universe in school. Space seemed to be such a big mystery. I remember wondering if scientists might one day discover that life existed far from earth. I have since used the same calm I had that night as a prelude to putting my thoughts into motion.

I realize now that I was able to enter into a calm because of my belief system. I believed I could have visions because I had them many times before. Gazing into space had allowed me to bring my emotions into a calm of pure concentration. I had blanked out everything around me. My focus and thoughts were centered only on space. I was thinking of life far out in the universe.

The night sky was the stage, so to speak, for my mind to generate thoughts to seek life in space. It was not so much that it had to be the skies to get my mind into a complete calm but the serenity of the calming sky. My mind easily slipped into another time when I sat in this serene setting viewing space. The space simply drew my mind into a vacuum that took my thoughts into another depth of time.

You might call this channeling and I suppose it was a parallel to that but to me, it was in the calm that my mind went beyond. I had no idea of what was about to happen although I can see why it did. My mind was free of any outside interference. I had traveled with my thoughts to a void into another world. Not being afraid and remaining calm was the key to what came next.

I remember that my thoughts were on life in space and now I know that I was really presenting a need for my answers about life in space. I also know now that these answers were not in space but actually from past memories that dwelled in my soul.

My first vision that night was what I know now to have been the energy fields in all of the colors of the rainbow. I recall it as being beautiful. As the colors swirled I felt myself being drawn into the moving circles of color. It was as if a door had opened and I was walking through it into another time. I felt that at that moment I really knew what space was like.

In this swirling energy I began receiving thoughts as if they were coming from somewhere in this space and time and what I heard became my thoughts. The vision began to change and I saw myself as a child. Not in my earthly setting but in another setting in another time. I instinctively knew I was that person living and breathing and I was the child speaking. It seemed that I was observing from a distance yet I became the little girl.

I watched for a long time as this little girl played and interacted with her friends. I did not hear her voice as I hear you. I only received the thoughts she had. It seemed a pleasant way to spend my time. My next awareness was that I had really fallen asleep. The cool night air had awakened me and the vision and thoughts I had were gone.

Was it a dream? I wondered, but it had seemed so real. Dreams are like that sometimes. What I experienced escaped back into my memories to draw on later. I knew I couldn't tell anyone for fear of being ridiculed again.

I have recalled that night many times in my search to direct my mind to my soul for answers. Because of what happened I knew there was a link between a calming state and seeking answers. I was not taunted by the fact that it may have all been a dream. The experience was pleasant and I re-entered this realm of peace many times. I have practiced this phenomenon many times to find visions as the years have gone by. In my experiences I have come to realize that there was another element called energy that I had used to transport thoughts.

This led me to research the presence of energy fields around us. In my adult years I discovered how energy plays a big part in our travels to our soul. Because I want you to dwell on my story and not how I was able to find my past memories in my soul, I want to explain how energy flows through the mind and soul forever.

The soul, which is the mind and spirit are all a form of energy. Think of them as a mass of energy held together with gases of their own energy forces forever. These forces coexist using the same energy forces within, to hold our memories.

As a child we are born with the energy flowing through within the spirit of life and to our mind and soul. With this in place at our birth, we rapidly formulate our thoughts. It is with the forces of energy within that we are linked with those energies that allow us to find our mind through our thoughts. Each of us is captured in a body that can use our own mind to allow us to have the freedom of thoughts. Our thoughts that are formulated are transported through the energy forces around and within us.

We have freewill so we must have something else that moves our thoughts through the energy forces to find those memories in our soul. What else could it be but our desire that begins the cycle to carry us into a higher realm of thought? The messages that I will deliver to you tonight are because of the energy that takes my thoughts into a different realm.

We are seated here in a quiet serene place where we can view the stars. The view is calming and allows me to shut out all outside noises, to have complete focus and concentration. My freewill allows me to search and my thoughts will seek answers that are deep within my soul. The energy forces are working for me because of my own desire that sets energy into motion.

Follow me with your mind so you too can grasp the process I am using. It is happening. I have moved my thoughts to a time in my past where I can see and hear the story of my own life in another time. My only road map is that I have a purpose in mind and that by learning of my past I can find answers for the present. This is the good that will come from it. My desire to find these answers is the key. The desire moves the energy and the process is set into motion. My desire is wrapped up in my belief and trust that my messages and visions will come. I am ready and I am seeking answers.

As my desire peaks, my mind is being transported into another realm of time. I can see deeper into my whole being. I am a part of this vision and yet I can see the visions are moving forward in my mind. I see space as a whole and God is present in this space that we are all part of.

I can now receive thoughts of knowledge that are moving me even deeper into myself. The vision comes to me. It is a picture of my own life being previewed by my own thoughts. In this space it is like being free from all human aspects of life and knowing that God is opening the door to new visions. I am now aware of things that I would not be aware of if I were not in this state of mind. It is knowledge that is given to me in thoughts that I do not challenge. It's like the information I am receiving has already been in my mind and now in this state I am aware of it.

This awareness that I feel is an experience in itself. Have you ever been in a situation when you have an urgency about something that is about to happen? You know it's going to happen and you know you must react to it quickly. It is like someone is telling you to become aware. My soul at this point is coming to me. These memories of the past dwell here. I am seeking out information. I am going to my soul for this knowledge of my past.

Think of this; there are two different reactions when you search into a new area with your mind. The two different reactions are going to and from the same place. The soul has a door that opens from two different directions. You can easily wait around for the information to come to you or you can stimulate your own thoughts with desire and become aware of the transport of thought to take you into your soul for the answers you are seeking.

You my friend will hear the messages from my lips as I relate my thoughts and visions of my past that are coming from my soul."

VISIONS

Richa's journey to Atlantis would be by land and sea.

ATLANTIS *A New View*

## ANCIENT ITALY

**Fields that were graced with the wisdoms of the past.
Paths to travel that would lead them to the freedoms that would last**

ATLANTIS *A New View*

## CHAPTER II:

## MEMORIES OF ITALY

It was a pleasure to be in Unique's company and I was anxious for her to tell her story. It was difficult to sit quietly in her garden, waiting for her to begin. My friend seemed content to be drinking in the view of the night sky around her. I tried to calm my own thoughts and absorb what she had told me about what she had been seeing and feeling.

My own gaze turned to the stars shining brightly in the sky. My thoughts traveled with Unique through space into another time as she began with a prayer thanking God for allowing her to reveal her past. She asked for God's guidance in telling the story in a way to expand the belief of others so they too could focus their minds into the depth of time. Unique's prayer was touching. I felt excitement for what she was about to tell me. I knew it was going to be a magical night.

Unique began speaking, **"This experience began in what we now call Italy, BC. It is difficult for me to pinpoint the exact date in history. My visions do reference a specific time but for the most part I am unable to put the exact date on the vision unless I can parallel the time with other historical happenings. The time I speak of is before the time of Moses. I believe it to be about 1400 BC I see a vision of Italy and it is beautiful. The hills are rolling and villages are scattered through out with land being farmed in between. I see vineyards very much like the vineyards of today but the farming tools are so different. I can see some curved blades with handles that look as if they have been handmade and hammered into shape. I take them to be tools for cutting weeds and** grasses.  Men are carrying them over their shoulders.  They also have what looks like a water buffalo loaded down with baskets hanging from either side of the animal's back.  I can see that they have stopped walking.  Women have joined the men and they are all picking grapes and putting them into the baskets.  It is a warm day and it looks like it is hard and tedious work."

Unique stopped talking abruptly and then said, **"This isn't going to work.  If I work strictly with the visions I am seeing now I can only relate to you what comes to me and they won't be in the order that would make my story complete.  Since finding memories from my past is something I have done for a very long time I think it would be better if I told you the whole story as I have pieced it together over the years.**

**I have gathered my information from the visions that have always come from a desire to know.  My mind has taken me into the depths of my soul to a particular time and degree to find my answers.  If what I desire are answers that pertain to what is good for the growth of the soul, then I am rewarded with excellent details.  If my desires could be considered only for my own benefit and for selfish reasons, then the visions are there but are indirect and often evasive.**

**It took me a long time to realize that what I desired in answers were sometimes only for my own benefit. I came to understand that even though the visions and thoughts were sometimes indirect to my desires they held many bonuses.  The bonuses were additional insights and were always colorful as well as interesting.  They were especially delightful when I learned personal things about the family.**

In reviewing these insights I can readily see that there was a purpose in having seen beyond my own interests. As an example, I have received information about other tribes and topography that did not pertain to the answers that I was seeking. I now believe these were insight messages that were given to me to pass on to others. The messages would be used because they were of a personal interest to others and it clarifies that particular time. The messages have become inspirational to search the soul for answers. I have passed on the potential for growth of the soul to many by passing on these messages that link with interests in areas other than mine. You will find because of this, my story includes everything that I have learned about this priestess.

One last thing before I begin; thoughts from our souls are meant to be understood but do not always come in ways that are easily interpreted. I may be telling my story from what I saw as a vision or symbolism but with no thoughts that came to me. Other visions include thoughts. Thoughts always come to me in English but sometimes mixed with phrases and words from another time. I know I am not interpreting incorrectly. The thoughts are revealed in a way that a new thought comes to clear up any misinterpretation.

Now, let me try again to tell my story from the beginning. Are you comfortable with what I have been telling you?"

I answered Unique's question with, "I am trying to stay calm but it is with great difficulty. Learning new insight to me is like receiving valuable messages that I could never receive in the same way that you do."

Unique continued, **"You are wrong about not being able to receive messages in the way that I do, but we will** get back to that later. I love sharing my experiences and I feel fortunate to have such a captivated audience.

I have watched over my namesake, Unique, with many trips into my past. The more I returned to this time of her life the more in depth the information became. I have always had this strange sensation of being a part of Unique as I watched her but not really a part of her. Her thoughts and personality seem to become my own as I see and hear her. She laughs easily and has a light heart, but as you will see, she takes her causes seriously."

Unique's face reflected from the light of the stars and I could see a broad smile as she said, **"You know, since in reality I am Unique and my story is about Unique in another time, it could be confusing if I do not make a distinction between both. To start this life around 1400 BC, her family gave her a lovely name of Richa but as she grew up she was often called, Priestess because of her ways. I shall follow through with calling her Richa, the name she was best known as. Richa means "the righteous one". You will see that Richa fits her pattern in life.**

My earliest visions were of Richa living with her family on a very large mass of land jutting into the ocean. This island, of sorts, lays along the eastern shore of Italy at the lower part of what we call the boot. It was land that was fertile for farming grapes and grains. The seas that surrounded it on three sides provided a plentiful supply of fish for eating and drying. One can see why Richa's family chose to settle there. They had left a nomadic way of life in northern Greece for a peaceful life style that provided for all of their needs of survival in one place.

## MEMORIES OF ITALY

Not all of Italy was settled in this way. It was not all a land of peace. Roaming tribes fought for their own type of peace and they controlled many parts of Italy. The tribes came from all parts of Europe. Some were nomadic and they wandered the hills and some tribes lived in small villages that were nestled among the hills. The villagers for the most part sought to live in peace. They protected themselves from intruders with rock walls.

Richa's family sought peace and chose to live by the spiritual values they carried with them. Their belief in God gave them a positive path to seek peace and to extend kindness to others. The family was made up of great storytellers and they spread their beliefs with the spoken word. They were centered on their own spirituality but they were not immune to the world around them. Often family members traveled to other villages and they brought stories back from others. Bartering and trading of produce and goods in local markets also brought communication with tribes from other parts of the world. One thing they all had in common was that they gladly shared their experiences. Story telling was an enjoyment and it often became the entertainment for those gathered around a fire as the daylight darkened into night.

Richa was considered a free spirit. Her family had a very large extended family that loved and sheltered their own from any harshness of the world around. In the safety of a families' love, Richa was given many freedoms. Being a curious child, she asked many questions and was always eager to open new doors of learning within and beyond her world.

Her parents taught her that a special spirit has the answers hidden deep within the mind and that allows one to know how to reach into those recesses for answers. I believe that Richa knew the process of going to the soul to find her answers. She found it was possible because it was a process that was wrapped up in trust and love.

She often used the stars for meditation. Watching the navigation of the stars set her mind at peace. It was a method she used so that her mind could reach deeper to reveal to her the belief of trust and love in a higher power. The spaces were awesome to her and moved her mind deeper into another time. As I followed her in meditation I was overcome by the trust she had in believing this was the path she could follow. She searched for answers from the visions and messages she had not known before.

I have pictured Richa as being the perfect example of following a spiritual life for fulfillment but it was not always so. I often heard her thoughts that were sometimes impetuous. She was full of an energetic force that burst with enthusiasm for the unknown. It often led her to the brink of challenging herself and boldly reaching out to others to hear of their travels and experiences. Richa sought to know the location of all the villagers and tribes around her with her incessant questions. There wasn't a village or a path she did not learn of as well as the people who lived or roamed there. She was especially keen to know of worldly places beyond. Many stories came to her about a place we now call Atlantis. She was totally fascinated with dreams of traveling to this island one day.

In spite of the fact that Richa was a woman in a man's world it was her boldness in communicating her visions and her stories to others that brought her respect. The knowledge that she acquired from the outside world was incredible. She was asked many questions but she was also a good listener and mentally took in everything she heard. She understood that life outside of her circle of life was very different. She knew that peace did not rein as it did on her island. There were many avenging villagers that led others into battle for fear of their lives. The only safety net they knew were their fortresses of rock that separated them from roaming tribes. She knew all of this yet she yearned to see the outside world for herself. It was obvious to those around her that she would not be satisfied until one day she could travel on her own.

From her family, Richa learned that it was not the fortresses that were built around the village that would bring them peace. It was in how to persuade others to believe in God that would be the solution from fear of each other. It was in that belief that groups were formed to find a better way to live among others in peace. They believed in using their own minds to convince others that kindness and love could prevail.

In the beginning it was a small colony of believers that taught others how God's ways came first. They were very much like an evangelist group. On their travels among villages they gathered with those that believed as they did. In this way they could spread out to worship with others. In this freedom of finding peace they could see clearly into their own missions and knew that others would become a part of their mission when they too could see that it was God they needed to rely on. In time many groups were formed and they taught that peace was found in following God's ways. It was in following those tactics that they believed they could all find peace among each other. Richa's association with these groups made it clear in her mind to pursue peace in the same way.

Having freedom and curiosity with the belief of God instilled within was a combination not unlike the children of today, except Richa lived in another time. The events in her life stemmed from her freedom of choice and she used this in chartering her own pattern in life. What I saw from Richa were lessons she learned when her parents held the responsibility of influencing the choices she would eventually take.

Richa's freedom allowed her thoughts to flow freely. In this way her thoughts easily brought on more thoughts. In her trust and belief in God, her thoughts soon brought with them visions. Her family's beliefs were passed on to her but she also carried the insight of knowing God's spirit in her soul. Her mind was open to what lay beyond. This freedom of the mind allowed her to find a way to see. Her family encouraged her and as she grew so did her visions.

In watching her, I felt that it was her sharing and caring that allowed her to preserve those thoughts for the stories she told. Preserving to her meant actually sharing all she knew with others. First in the stories she told because she had good listeners. And then in her strength of her resolve to find more visions and to look in other ways to describe what she was seeing. I can only wonder if what she saw was the basis of her creativity or if the creativity was because of her family's support. Perhaps it was both.

Nevertheless, in time as Richa grew to become a young lady she discovered she could strengthen other's beliefs in what she saw with symbolic art. By now I had watched her move through many periods of her life. She did not attend school in the traditional way of today but she learned a lot over the years. She was sheltered and yet she learned the ways of survival just as any child of today.

Food and shelter were a part of survival. She knew the importance of being protected from the elements. She lived with her family in huts made of rocks and clay that cut the winds and the cold. She learned how to gather grain and fruits and how to fish from the sea. She was taught how to dry and store food for eating and bartering.

All that she learned was as automatic as the years that slipped by. I could hear the same voices that came to her when she was in deep thought and I saw what she was seeing. I could not interfere in any way. It was almost always like a dream world that I was watching except that through her thoughts I shared her world. I felt her joys and her concerns. I felt the same urges she had in being creative and her eagerness to learn. Her dreams of travel became my own dreams. I too desired to see Atlantis.

I was transfixed at her openness to share. She was serious but also childlike in her trust of others. Her visions were a constant reminder to her of the love of God. They gave her the desire to create objects of art that would be useful but would also show God's love. I could hear and understand the thoughts coming from her mind with ideas to make her visions come to life. In her desire to be creative Richa turned to the beauty that surrounded her. She became engulfed in making creations that would inspire others to see the wonders that God could reveal. She sensed she was close to God by the love she felt. It was like a light that went on in her mind as she gathered new thoughts. She realized that her creations would have to be looked upon by others as symbols of the miracles that God presents.

With purpose, Richa looked around her small world to find objects that would express what she was seeing and thinking. To my delight she saw the grapes in vineyards as more than a fruit to eat and juices to drink. She saw gnarled wood that held beauty only if she could fashion articles that symbolized love. She saw the vines that wound around the massive trunks as a way to put her ideas into their own visions to tell a story. She used the cast off gnarled wood of the pruned grape trunks to make staffs. She was not the first one to find uses for a staff, as she had seen many times the shepherds using them to gather their herds or for others using them as a walking stick. She envisioned making the staffs ornate in a way that would have a spiritual and meaningful symbol of love. At first her creations were simple. The staffs were cut from grape stocks and were carefully embellished with vines entwined around the stock. They were useful as walking sticks, but most important the villagers saw the beauty from the love instilled in her creations. Soon she was adding bright colored pebbles to delight the villagers. Her staffs began to take on individuality depending on how she crafted them.

Her family encouraged her to place her creations for bartering in the local market. She became a regular figure at the market selling her staffs. Along with trading her staffs she shared stories of her visions with all that would listen. It was not long that both her creativity in the staffs and the stories of her visions spread.

# MEMORIES OF ITALY

Just as creativity finds more creativity she was soon seeking to incorporate what she knew of art with what the ancients used before her time. She was looking for a way that would send the mind into a calmness to find answers.

Her mind warmed to the thought of presenting the villagers with articles that could relieve their stress of the times. She made beads like those of ancient origins that allowed her to find the proper sequence. It was like the beads the Catholics use today. The stones that became part of her art were soon known to relieve others from the stress of their own times. The rocks and crystals she used were carved in shapes that could be held and circulated freely in the hands. They were looked at as a reflection of light that could help the mind see clearly.

She could take the bead whether it was small or large and place it in the hands of those that would reach out. They knew that they had been touched by tranquility and would start believing in her ways. Richa found this response to be her answer for stimulating minds into believing in God's ways. It was like a confirmation that encouraged her to create more articles of art.

A pattern was developing for Richa. Her faith was inspiring others. Was it irony or destiny that she met many priests who traveled in her time? They came from many places; they shared in the love of God, but they also brought with them many stories of the outside world. They lingered near Richa's station at the market to hear her stories but mostly she listened to what they had to share. What she heard from priests not only strengthened her own beliefs in God and the purpose for her art, but it opened her awareness to follow her own dream.

Richa was by now in her early twenties. She was lovely in a special way. Her hair was long and flowing and her body tall and strong. She was a beauty in motion but it was her face that held the magic. Her features were soft and her dark eyes held the attention of others as she told her stories. She remained unattached to a love of her own except for her family and the dreams she had to travel. Her relationship with God had put her into a pattern that allowed her to frequent the times spent with priests. It was from their stories that she learned the most and formed her own convictions that would lead her adventurous mind on. She took up the dress code of the priests. Her robes were of dark cloth and fell loosely around her. It was her way of melting in with the other priests. Perhaps she felt it was in tune with her beliefs as a priestess.

Richa heard frightening stories but the most frightening was about the people of Atlantis. She learned from others of the perils that lurked there but she never wavered in her desire to find a way to see for herself. She realized there was danger in being absorbed in their beliefs if the mind melted into following the same path of cruelty. She felt she was strong enough in her own convictions and could stay without the grasp of anything evil happening to her. In this area of trust she was certainly unaware of all the dangers and it was the boldness of youth speaking.

The possibility of visiting Atlantis was talked about by many. The villagers knew of others that had ventured to Atlantis and did not come back as the same people that left. They were stern in their thinking in that it was the drugs of Atlantis that would be the downfall of all. They believed that in time it would have to be God's own rapture that would produce the downfall of Atlantis.

Richa was driven and yet divided in her thoughts. She was close to her own family ties and did not want to change that interaction. She decided to pray for her decision about Atlantis. There were many friends and family members that did not agree with her decision to go but she was convinced in her own mind that God would protect her in this venture. She did not realize that God had given her freewill to make choices and in following her own desires, she might not be choosing a path that was safe for her life.

She generated a lot of energy to calm the fears of those concerned about her. She was a walking encyclopedia on the do's and don'ts and the risks she was taking. The knowledge she had gained from listening to others was the mastery she used in moving others to accept her ways. She was not a boat person but she knew the direction and paths by heart that would be helpful on such a journey. She possessed the knowledge of many and reiterated it again and again for others to follow closely. She was eager to please, but was dedicated and eager to expand on the knowledge of Atlantis that she had found to be so fascinating.

Richa understood that the trip to Atlantis would have to be taken both by land and by sea. She cast aside all of her doubts and was eager to venture into such a trip of this magnitude. She spent many hours discussing the trip with a group of men she knew. She tried to implant her own thinking into this small group that she would be traveling with. Her rhetoric sometimes reached highs and lows with her own enthusiasm. Many in the group did not understand her moods but were fascinated with the way she could adjust her thinking to overcome their own doubts. She managed to convince them that they truly needed her expertise because of her knowledge. In the end they were convinced that she was indeed the party that would allow them to follow the right trails and they offered her a position to travel with them.

Excitement grew among this small group. They knew of the risks in traveling on their own and understood there would be trials on the trails. Among the small group was experienced boats men, but they knew that the seas were treacherous and bravery was not always enough to overcome a quick storm that would surely rise in a sea of waves. They knew all of this but they also shared Richa's desire to view the island of Atlantis for themselves. It was with eagerness that this small group made plans to proceed, but they had many things to overcome in the way of preparation.

Being properly equipped for a land trip of this type was easy because most of them had done it many times, but not so when it came to traveling by sea. The first obstacle was in finding a seaworthy boat large enough for a journey that would take many weeks. It looked as though finding a boat would be more than finding the nearest harbor that boats regularly sailed in and out of. Most boat people with larger crafts were traders and followed their own trade routes. They knew of Atlantis but because of the dangers that existed, there were some that were afraid to include that route into their own. Those that did go that way had no room for passengers.

I watched Richa work through this obstacle coarse with a determination that I had not seen her possess before. She retained her trust and love in God but it was as if she was possessed with Atlantis and those thoughts filled her life. There was no family member or friend that was able to deter her from her determination to put her travel into action. Between my visits into Richa's past I too wondered if she would indeed succeed in her determination to put this adventure together."

ATLANTIS *A New View*

## SEA MERCHANTS

They owned the high seas with the maneuvers that took them far off land to not be seen.
They mastered their crafts and were poised for the water with their bodies strong and lean.
They were known for their wisdoms and their senses that were forever keen.

ATLANTIS *A New View*

## CHAPTER III:

## A JOURNEY INTO THE UNKNOWN

It was strange listening to Unique tell the story of her past life in Italy. She was so intense with describing Richa's determination to go to Atlantis that it sent shivers up my spine. I felt the power of Unique's voice as if it was wrapped up in the power of Richa's voice

Unique went on with her story. **"Richa set about convincing a small group of her friends that it would be advantages if she were to accompany them to Atlantis. It wasn't until after she got them to agree that they needed her knowledge of Atlantis, that they began to consider how they could find a boat. The fact that none of them had a boat to travel by sea did not deter Richa's enthusiasm from finding a way to overcome yet another obstacle.**

**At first it seemed to me that what Richa had accomplished in agreements with the others to allow her to travel with them was for naught. Obstacles were nothing new to Richa and she set about with her usual determination. If there were boats to be had she would find one that would take them to Atlantis. I watched her use a systematic process by visiting every family member who had anything to do with trade on the sea. This took days to go from one family member to another but Richa never wavered. In the end she found that one from her own group, Leonardo, who was the key that would allow them to find a passage on a boat to Atlantis.**

**Leonardo was someone Richa had known all of her life. She saw him as the patient one in her family's group, who did not speak a lot but carried with him the**

wisdom that drove others to maintain peace. His family was made up of merchants and they had connections that extended far. It included a merchant uncle on the western coast of Italy. He confided in Richa that his uncle had a large Persian trading boat and wanted him to set up trade with Atlantis. He had been harboring those thoughts for a long time, but did not think it would be possible to take up roots and join his uncle.

I called it stacking the deck but to Richa it was a sound proof idea to accomplish a task she could not do by herself. I watched her manipulate her friend Leonardo, into accepting the challenge to set up the trade route and include her small group of friends as passengers. I was excited as I saw the transformation of this small group come together.

They all had the same dream to go to Atlantis but they each had different reasons. There were five in the group of which one was Richa. They were all of her friends that had known her from the beginning. The group consisted of Leonardo, Richa, Federico, Mikus and Baylona in all.

The priest among them was Mikus who had studied long and hard to become a priest. He descended from those that were Greek and did not take up his own calling until he met up with those that taught him the calling of what I believe to be Hindu. It was in that calling that Mikus observed many facets of God's ways that warmed his own desire to live his life in ways that he could follow along. He had his own personal calling to go to Atlantis in hopes of helping those find a better way of life.

Federico also had his own calling to be a priest. He wanted to help others but he also wanted the challenges that he knew lay ahead.

# A JOURNEY INTO THE UNKNOWN

Baylona was the rugged one in his own ways. He was a frontiersman of sorts and took notice of his surroundings for any dangers that lurked. He could spot a trail from far away. He also knew the challenges ahead in providing food and water. He seemed to be a man who would take no guff from those that would dilly-dally along the way. He was structured to march in formation and would be looking out for any dangers in the bushes ahead.

This small group held the thrill seekers and the curious but they also carried with them their own spiritual beliefs. Richa believed that God would be their protection through out their whole journey. There were many religious differences among the group but that did not seem to matter because they allowed each to believe in their own way.

It would be a two-week journey to the western coastal village where the boat was harbored. The terrain they would pass over would be sometimes mountainous and the trail would not always be clear to follow. They would also have to be aware of marauders who preyed on travelers to steal food and to kill anyone in their way.

Richa set about with the help of the other members of the group to prepare for the journey overland. There were plenty of breads, dried fruits and vegetables and even meats to pack for the overland trip. The problem was that a caravan using pack animals would not work because of the treacherous trails, so this meant that they would be traveling on foot.

Their food and water would be limited with what they could carry. They would be looking at the expertise of Baylona to help them find food along the way. Baylona trusted in nature to provide and they were always pleasantly surprised at his knowledge of Mother Nature. He was the kind that could make a full course meal from finding berries and small animals that he could capture with his own hands. He would mystify them all in his own creative talents that would always please their pallets. They would find Baylona indispensable for their survival.

As I relate this story to you I want you to know that I returned time and time again to my past memories to follow Richa and the others to their destination across the land. I watched as they shared many experiences with each other over the two weeks it took to trek first southerly and then westerly over the trails to the western coast of Italy.

I have called this area southern Italy so you can visualize the topography when in fact this part of the world was called Oenotrust at that time. It was named by a colony from Arcadia (Greece) that settled in South Italy in 1710-B.C. It was much later that Oenotrust became Italy. Also, you need to know that Italy, as we know it now, did not look the same as in Richa's time. The time we are visiting was around 1400 BC and Italy was a much larger landmass than it is today. It had a somewhat different shape, especially along the coasts. As an example, the heel of the boot was much wider. What we know as Sicily had a much closer connection to the main landmass of Italy. Huge earthquakes since Richa's time have devastated many of the inlets and shore lines leaving many lost lands in the wake of the sea. I mention this because as the group traveled across country I don't want you to think of it the way the maps portray it today.

It was a long and tiring trek but the group made the most of the time on the trail. Each one quickly found a close kinship to each other and linked together as one. They shared their own passions that had joined them together in the first place to take such a journey. Their most common thread was their eagerness to see Atlantis. It was interesting to watch the group interact with all of those that they met along the way and to listen to the others tell their own stories of other journeys. Even Baylona, who was the marcher, became absorbed with the people along the way and was found to encourage the stops.

At one place on the trail they met with families that had taken up roots and were traveling to find a better pasture. There were also hunters along the way that had their own calling to roam about to study the animals so that they could find ways to domesticate them for others to use. The group did meet with marauders on occasion but were happy to be passed by. They were avoided because they were looked at as a holy group with Mikus, the priest, leading the way.

I anticipated they would have trouble finding water along the way but that was not so. Baylona knew of the wells and the streams that flowed freely. They were also traveling at a time of year that the streams were flowing with clear water from the mountains above. With plenty of water they all felt that God had really sanctioned their journey and was looking out for them.

What impressed Richa the most were the children on the trail that journeyed with their own families to find new homes. The children were eager to show Richa that they responded well to changes and were happy to play along the way. They did not seem to care where their own placement led them. They only knew that their own families cared for them in a special way and they were happy to tag along wherever the family took them. Watching Richa relate to the children was a fascinating view. Even with her determination and high spirit to get on to Atlantis, it was the children that held her mind in a special calm. I think she was reminded of her own childhood and the protection of her own family no matter what the situation was.

Our travelers also encountered soldiers along the way that were lame from having fought wars. They now were searching for their own families. It was with great sadness that I saw men that were crippled and were moving slowly along on foot. They had battled long and hard to keep the peace within their own lands. In the struggle their families had been split and had wandered about looking for a more promising place to live. It was the determination in their eyes that they would one day find their loved ones that stayed with me as I watched the group continue.

One of the most fascinating evenings spent on the trail was when the group met up with those that had already stepped foot on Atlantis. They were full of stories about Atlantis that they had seen first hand. Through those eyes and the stories, the group found excitement that added to their own desire to view Atlantis for themselves.

They heard of the beauty of the island on one hand but also of the evil that was destroying souls and keeping them in harms way because of greed. They heard of the laboratories where animal parts were attached to human bodies for strength. They were told that bodies were thrown into the sea if one of the experiments did not work out the way they had intended. They had heard of the starvation of the animals that they were using for their evil ways. The stories were overwhelming and pointed to the masterminds on the island of Atlantis that were causing it to self-destruct. Their evil plan was to break down the justices of others and use them for their own power. Atlantis was clearly an island of beauty in the land but it was being turned into a kingdom of hell. The group was saddened but their determination to see for themselves stayed with them.

The days were long and hard, but they remained a giving group that was always willing to share what little they had brought along. When they approached a village, the villagers were eager to replenish them with food or materials that they could use to go on. The villagers trusted them all, especially since they were with Mikus, the priest. In their eyes, they also saw Federico take on the role of a priest when they found he was studying to be one.

The villagers enjoyed the talents of Baylona, who instructed them on how to find food. He also questioned anyone who had covered the trail they were on about the kind of food they could watch for. It was a great exchange between travelers and villagers helping each other.

Leonardo was a joy with his patience and calm that held the group together and in control of a peaceful time along the way. I could see that Richa's role changed somewhat from the organizer of the group in the beginning to a position more in tune as a traveling companion. She offered a perspective of her own with her stories. She was looked at in praise to have journeyed on such a trek but mostly for the kindness she showed those along the way. She listened well to others and these insights brought her closer to finding new ways to capitalize on. Sharing her thoughts left others with their own insights along the way. She had great knowledge of all those places that she found to be part of her own spectrum of knowledge. She had a unique way of expressing herself that led others to find their own stories to share. It was inspirational to hear the exchanges and to see how each storyteller grew in their ability to pass on their own messages.

As the days went by the group wound their way along the trail continuing in a westerly direction toward the far shores of Italy. Late one day it was Mikus that shouted out to the others that the sea was just ahead. I was watching Richa as she caught up with Mikus and captured her first view of the coast. I felt her warmth from the thanks she was feeling. Mikus raised his hands in an outpouring of thanks to God. Richa followed with hands uplifted as did the others. There was jubilation in the camp that night for having had a safe journey overland. In celebration Baylona caught fresh fish from the sea and prepared it in his own special way to feast on. It was a merry sight to watch them eat and rejoice.

It was Baylona that was up early the next morning. He was back to commanding and insisted that they quickly continue their march along the shores. His calculation was that they were less than half a day journey to the village where the boat was moored. He was right; in a very short time as they walked along the coast they had the village in their sight. To their delight they saw that there were many boats moored in a harbor close to shore.

It was a sight to remember as Federico sought out his uncle. Everyone in the village knew his uncle by the name, "Captano". There was merriment in the greetings of each other and acceptance of the others as if they were all old friends. The entire village rallied together in celebration. It was a feast like no other with a variety of foods the group had not had since they left home. They shared stories into the night, mostly about Atlantis.

In the harbor, as if it was waiting for the group was the boat they would be taking to Atlantis. I was astonished at how small it looked compared to the boats we have today. The group took in the view of the boat with excitement. They did not have a concern about the size of the boat; it was pure happiness that they now had the means to sail out of the harbor toward Atlantis. They all knew that the boat would carry goods for trading and there would be many stops along the way, but this was part of the excitement.

I have been calling what I saw a boat; but in the mind of Richa and the others it was a vessel. It had been hand crafted in Persia. It was strongly built to carry cargo for trading. Although it was Persian built, it looked almost Viking like in appearance. If you have ever seen pictures of a trireme vessel of this period you would know there were places for many oarsmen on each side. This vessel was smaller with only places for eight oarsmen. There were strong masts with sails that they would use in the open seas. There would be a crew of three more besides the oarsman plus Captano and the group of five excited friends. There were seventeen in all. The vessel was not built as a passenger vessel so the small group of friends would have to ride in the helm. It would be a very small space but the tight quarters did not bother them.

The oarsmen were thrilled at the challenges that took them into strange waters. They were eager to see the island of Atlantis and hoped it would lead them to a new trade line. They were seasoned oarsmen and could maneuver the oars in a special way through the strong currents.

The cargo was to consist of many spices and teas that they had heard that the Atlantis people craved. They also had carvings aboard from their own families that they could sell to the coastal and island people on the way. The carvings were statues depicting scenes that all could enjoy from places they may have come from or would like to be reacquainted with.

To survive they would take plenty of dried fruits and the meat of sheep as well as bread from the grains they had grown at home. They carried with them a supply of water that would last for seven days. They would replenish by catching rain water as often as possible. With the many stops along the way they could also replenish their supply of water. The food they carried with them would be sustaining but it was the feasts they would be treated to as they docked at different ports that excited them. Merchants were one of a kind. They saw their port dockings as a huge arena where they could feast and laugh and converse with each other.

Captano was a big rugged man that had a soft place in his heart for his nephew Leonardo, but he was also a merchant with an eye for the trades. His nephew would set up the link of trade to Atlantis. Leonardo would set up the pattern of trade so that they could launch trips back and forth along the way. Aside from business, it was Mikus the priest that inspired Captano the most to lead them with God safely on their way. Richa was established as wise in her own ways but not the leader.

The day came when I watched the vessel slowly move out into the currents. I would have liked to figure out their exact route but it was Mikus the priest, and

## A JOURNEY INTO THE UNKNOWN

Captano who were in charge and I was not always able to hear their conversations through Richa. The thoughts I picked up as I watched Richa were serene and she had complete trust in the hands that were directing the vessel. She sat in the helm to stay out of the way and enjoy the voyage. She did not take any articles of art with her but related well to those merchants that held art for others in their hands. She did carry a few beads of protection. She believed if she carried a few beads from her own homeland it would show her God's light and keep her safe until she would again return.

I smile at how well I had learned Richa by now. Her stories were her gift and she told many to all. She was also on a quest even while at sea. She believed some of the best stories came from merchants about the sea. It was a way for her to learn of the many places they had been. She was amazed at how the sea could swallow them up and spit them out to find another shelter.

The oarsman took them into the main currents to follow a channel between what we now know as Italy and Sicily. As far as the eye could see it was like a large bay with many inlets of sorts that jetted out from the shore. The waters looked like an island of itself that spread out to the sea. They crossed this channel many times on their route toward Atlantis. The route took them along the coast and around some small islands. Captano and his seamen believed tyrants of the sea lived deep in the water along the coast of Greece and they planned to avoid them at all cost. The plan was to follow the coast of Italy along the toe and the coastal area to the heel. This would protect them from the sea and the stops for trading would establish their desired trade route to Atlantis.

## ATLANTIS *A New View*

    As the days passed they docked at islands along the way. The merchants rode themselves hard as they bartered their goods. The stops each held many merchant stalls grouped together to display and share. I found it interesting that there was such a variety of wares from many places over the world. They met up with many that had come from the orient with their teas and wines. The Spaniards were at every stop and had brought gold pellets and an array of products from many places. They had silks and jewels as well as seaweed to trade. There were greedy merchants that everyone watched out for. They treated the seas like it was their own and no one else could sail before they gave the OK. They stood out among all of those that our group met. They kept a distance from our group because of Mikus the priest. They were wary of his power.
    Richa felt that it would be forever before they finally struck out across the open seas from the heel of Italy, but the day did come. The journey was during the summer months and they would arrive at Atlantis long before the fall weather came in. There was occasional rain but it only added to their own collection of cool water that they drank while out at sea.
    It was a straight shot out to sea from the heel of Italy. They used the setting of the sun and the moon and stars to follow their own maps along the way. They encountered no storms at sea and headed in an easterly direction. It was weeks later that they arrived to what they called the Keyes and Atlantis was among them. I know that I have not pin pointed the exact location of Atlantis, but I do realize from what I learned from Richa that Atlantis existed south of Thera and north of Crete.

## A JOURNEY INTO THE UNKNOWN

    As I watched the vessel with the group aboard, they set their sails to continue pretty much in an easterly direction and then one day Atlantis was sighted. I had my first glimpse through the eyes of Richa and what a sight that was. The island appeared to be huge. As they approached they could see that the coast was a place of great beauty. There seemed to be no end to its size, as the green land mass disappeared into the horizon. My own excitement grew as I watched through Richa's eyes."

# ATLANTIS *A New View*

My first glimpse of Atlantis through the eyes of Richa was an amazing experience.

# CHAPTER IV:

## FIRST GLIMPSE OF ATLANTIS

I was mesmerized at Unique's story. We had been sitting in the garden for many hours but it seemed like only a short time. In the light from the moon I could see that Unique's gaze remained on the stars. Her voice was mellow and calm. I knew from what she had told me that she was actually reliving those messages that she received from within. As she told her story her mind was with Richa. My attention was transfixed on Unique as she continued her story.

**"As the vessel sailed in closer to the island of Atlantis, the sails came down and the oarsmen took over to pull in toward the shore. The big island was nestled among other smaller islands that they had already passed. Richa knew that Captano was searching for a channel that would take them inside the island. She knew that there were many smaller islands in the area of Atlantis but she did not know that they were this close to the Atlantis shores.**

**Richa and the others watched as they got closer to see a long strip of sandy beach. There were people walking along the beach. They appeared to be beach combing. Nearby the group spotted a majestic fountain of water spilling out of the hills and flowing toward the depths of the ocean. There were many separate water falls and mist rose all around as the water fell thousands of feet to a pool then flowed out into a larger stream on its way to disappear in the ocean. The rock structures that were protruding along the falls and down to the sea took on their own formation. The water fell as if in arches over the massive rock across the beach to find the right**

harbor that allowed the flow to pass on. They were in awe watching the water move into one direction and then liquefy into a bigger pool and then disappear.

Along the sides of the falls was foliage. It was greenery that Richa had never seen before. The colors of the leaves were florescent in the breeze and she couldn't help staring. There were many more colors throughout the foliage. There were the green, red, and yellow lines mixed in with lavender and gold and royal purple. The foliage was massive in size and melted into the flowers that hung low on some of the leaves below. It looked like a jungle of today, except the array of colors were in a mass that scattered and intertwined around each other as if they belonged together. It was like taking all of the auras of the souls and melting them together to represent a mass that becomes a place to flourish and flower. The purple flowers spun out of control covering areas in masses as if they had their own pocket.

Soon the oarsmen were pulling the vessel close enough in to shore that they could distinguish the birds in flight. They were made up of all sizes and colors. Richa could not hear the birds over the roar of the falls but imagined that each had their own music with melodies that would be different and yet all blend together as one.

Captano saw an open channel along the beach from the falls. It was a very wide channel of water and had been obscured from their view because of all the foliage on both sides. The current was strong and it took all of the strength the oarsmen could muster but they slowly pulled the vessel into the channel. After a short fight with the turbulent water that flowed through the channel, the oarsmen pulled the vessel into the calm of a harbor.

# FIRST GLIMPSE OF ATLANTIS

The harbor was more than a harbor to hold a few vessels. As far as the eye could see there was a huge body of water that surrounded yet another mass of land in the center. I compared what I was seeing in Atlantis as having the shape of a doughnut. The hole of the doughnut was a landmass with water all around and only one channel opened from the sea to get to the inside harbor. On the inside ring of the island we could see a massive structure of stone. It had been perfectly described to Richa and the others as the castle of Atlantis. This was the place that the rulers of the island sat up their own fortress. The boulders that held it together were massive and of earthen colors. The size of the structure for this century of time was impressive. The structure was near the waters edge. There was no beach in this area. The castle seemed to hang over the water and on both sides of huge rocks that jutted out into the harbor.

Stretching out along the shores near the castle were smaller structures made of the same earth tone rocks. These structures also hung out over the water's edge. There were many. Richa wondered if these were the laboratories of the evil.

Our oarsmen continued to row their vessel through the harbor to a place along the outer ring of the island. The oarsmen soon rowed the vessel through a smaller channel that had Rocks jutting out on either side. The group could see that another huge harbor was opening up. Many vessels of all sizes and shapes dotted the water in this harbor. On the shore, the beach gradually sloped down to the water's edge with a huge mountain rising behind the beaches. The mountain was covered with thick foliage and seemed to extend up to the mountain as far as the eye could see. As the group drew closer they could see that for the most part the vessels that were moored there were all trading vessels. They did not recognize several Spanish vessels that they knew were used for pirating the seas. There was a huge market place spread out along the beach. People were moving about everywhere. They could see that there were venders hocking their goods and others tending fires and still others were watching them approach.

Richa was not surprised to see people of all origins through out the market area. After all Atlantis was recognized as one of the largest trading centers for merchants from many places. I would find the races that were represented here were as far away as the Bearing Sea to the North and the lands in between. What I know now as Africa and India was represented as well. There were many people from areas along the Mediterranean coast, Egypt and Africa. All were dressed in their own country's descriptive garments. One could recognize the aura of colors to be of fine silks. It was a sight to behold.

The stalls were heaped with everything imaginable. There were exotic flowers, fruits and vegetables that amazed Richa. She had never seen such a display of choices and neither had the others. The market was like a paradise of plenty, all laid out for bartering. There was a warm sea breeze blowing and it carried with it the smell of fresh flowers and mixed fresh fruits. Women were moving about with baskets of breads and oil for anyone who wanted to partake. There was fresh fish from the sea on display as well as fish and hunks of lambs cooking on open fires. She could see stalls gleaming with gold and silver goblets and trinkets shining from their displays. The crafts and wares were everywhere. Richa was

## FIRST GLIMPSE OF ATLANTIS

amazed at the creativity of the crafts in such a place. She spotted the pottery and knew immediately that she could learn new techniques. This was indeed the largest market place they had ever seen. The view brought excitement to the entire group.

    Captano's excitement was heard in his voice as he gave instructions to his oarsmen to pull in close for mooring. He could visualize that his vessel could become a new kind of merchant ship with exotic merchandise to trade. He saw items that he never dreamed existed. Captano and Leonardo grasped hands in merriment at the prospectus of establishing a new trade route. Baylona was taking in the market place with an eye for the exotic foods and spices that he was not familiar with. The gleam in his eyes and the big smile on his face told its own story of all the new possibilities these foods presented to him for a different kind of feast. Mikus, Federico and Richa scanned the market scene with enthusiasm but their eyes soon lifted to the mountain behind the market place and the trail they could catch sight of. They knew this trail would wind its way to the top. At the end of this trail would be their destination and they savored the thought of finding priests living there. They knew the priests had their own visions and their own answers but they knew they would be welcomed in as a part of their group. It was understood that a priest's life is in sharing with others. Our three were anxious to move on up the trail but first things first. They joined hands for a prayer of thanks for a safe journey and then they made plans to spend a night on the beach, feasting with their fellow travelers.

    Baylona set about setting up a camp site and supplying it with unusual fruits and meats that he had bartered for. Without a lot of fanfare the small group was soon feasting on the shores of Atlantis with thanks in their hearts. They shared this last feast before each took up their own plans. Captano and Leonardo along with Baylona and the same crew and oarsmen would be making regular trips from their homeland to and from Atlantis. Captano agreed to contact Richa, Mikus and Federico each time he arrived at Atlantis so that one day the small group of three would return with him to Italy.

Richa was light at heart that night as she anticipated the steep mountain climb to find a place in the home of the priests. She knew they could help her set up her own plans. She also knew that she must become part of this place to learn all of its secrets and why so many were changed when they reappeared back to their homeland. In spite of the anticipation of the next day Richa knew there was much to learn from others that were at hand. She moved to join her fellow travelers at a campfire encircled with many others all wanting to hear of their travels and to share in their own experiences.

As Richa made her way closer to the campfire she pulled the collar of her long robe around her head so she would not be recognized as a woman and could better melt into the group. As she looked around the campfire she realized that there were beggars on Atlantis. She had not noticed them in the market place when the group arrived and wondered why there was poverty on an island of plenty. This would be a question she would ask the priests.

The campfire burned brightly into the night as our group was given front stage to share their stories. Richa knew that there were language barriers among them and not everything could be understood. It did not seem to matter. The storytellers only got more verbal along with using their arms and facial expressions to demonstrate their stories. In this atmosphere there was simple enjoyment in sharing experiences.

It was not a surprise to the others in her own group to see Richa take her turn to tell a story and at the same time boldly lower her collar from around her head. It brought a few gasps from the crowd when they saw that she was a woman. The crowd got quiet as she began speaking but soon joined in again in merriment. Richa had a clever way of telling a story as she always got participation from the others and so it was this night. She asked Captano to stand beside her and together they talked of the vessel and how the journey on the seas began. Before they were done Richa had the entire group standing with her including the oarsmen and crew. It was like a stage show of today as each one in her group participated in telling of their experiences along the way.

Finally the fire was burning down to small embers and Richa moved closer to say good night. It was Mikus and Federico that escorted Richa back to the vessel where they would all spend their last night aboard. Richa saw these two priests as protectors and was thankful for their presence in this strange land.

Nobody slept well because of all the excitement. It was early the next morning that the group was up and moving about on shore. They were each anxious to get on with their day. Baylona was excited too about his own plans but he set about preparing the early meal as usual. He had an abundance of fresh fruits and cooked fish and warm bread. After eating, the group stood in a last lingering conversation with each other. It was sadness to say goodbye to the others but easier in another way because they knew they would one day see each other again.

    Richa, Mikus and Federico set out walking up the mountain trail. They peered into the foliage along the way as they walked because they had been warned of the wild animals and snakes that roamed there. They were told to especially watch out for the black and yellow snakes. They were deadly and lived among the masses of shrubs and overgrowth along the way. It was difficult to imagine how dangerous the trail could be when there was nothing but beauty on both sides of their path. They caught occasional glimpses of monkeys and could hear their chatter as if the three were disturbing their peace. As they walked they got a closer look at the purple flowers growing in masses along the path. These were the same kind of flowers that they had seen on the approach to the island. The flowers were actually delicate blooms but it was the masses of purple color that had made them stand out from afar.

    The three were in good physical shape from their journey and walked steadily upward along the path for a long length of time. They could see the sun higher and higher in the sky and felt the warmth and moisture from the tropical like jungle on either side. Richa finally felt the need for a rest. She was in the lead and spotted a large flat boulder along the path that seemed to be beckoning. She sat down and both Mikus and Federico followed suit.

    I have to tell you that seeing and hearing all of this through Richa's thoughts was fantastic. It reminded me of a video one could watch and hear with pure pleasure without being in the middle of any discomfort.

# FIRST GLIMPSE OF ATLANTIS

The three were resting and looking at the view back down to the harbor when a man approached them walking down the trail from above. He spoke and greeted them warmly in their own language. As they turned to face him he smiled. He was dressed in a long brown robe. He was a priest and he had come down the trail to meet them.

The three stood in respect of the priest but he motioned for them to sit back down and squatted on the ground along the other side of the trail to face them. He told them his name was Kaluba. I thought it was an unusual name. Richa, as usual, was full of questions and asked Kaluba how he knew they were coming. He told them that nothing takes place on this island without one of the priests coming back to make a report.

Kaluba told them that they still had the steepest part of their trek to travel yet. They should take some nourishment from the bread and meat he had brought along and with the cool water he carried in a skin bag at his side. It was not difficult to see that such kindness promoted an instant friendship on the side of the mountain.

Kaluba in his loose brown robe looked very much like the robes the others were wearing. One could not help noticing a softness of caring etched in his face that spelled trust. The group was soon to learn that he also was a great storyteller. He seated himself on a rock looking back down the mountain as he swept his outstretched hand in a gesture across the view below and proceeded to tell them of the beginnings of Atlantis.

Kaluba spoke with an accent but it did not prevent the three from understanding him. The language did not matter to me as all my thoughts from Richa were

## ATLANTIS *A New View*

received and translated into English. I could hear Kaluba easily through Richa as he said," *"Atlantis came from the sea from great rumblings and forces pushing up the ground until Atlantis was formed in the roughest of rock and soil. This was many years ago. From this beginning came the vegetation that you now see. Growth was encouraged easily in this climate because of the warmth and the moisture of a jungle like atmosphere. On this mountain a great amount of moisture is formed that leaves an early morning mist over everything.*

*The large island arose from the sea with huge quakes. From the beginning this mass of land was surrounded by a body of water. It was in that body that other channels found their own courses and many small islands appeared. All of the islands are lush with tropical growth springing from everywhere as you have seen. Each mass of land is surrounded by water that flows freely. And so Atlantis is truly a mass of many spread out.*

*The first human life to come to this island was of the ancients that were descendents of warriors. They were dictators in their own right and found their way to Atlantis as rulers to glorify their new way. They wanted to control the earth. They were warriors themselves and came from the land north of Italy. I am sure you have heard of them from the stories of Atlantis' beginning. They were escaping to find their own freedoms and looked at these lands in the sea as a place to set up their own kingdoms."*

"As I listened through Richa I got the distinct impression that Kaluba was talking about the homeland of the warriors that is now Switzerland. I knew questions would come and was not disappointed when I heard Richa asking question after question until Kaluba raised his hand." *"All of your answers will come in good time.*

## FIRST GLIMPSE OF ATLANTIS

*One must learn to be patient. Our first dwellers on this island knew that this island existed because of the stories that came back from those traveling on the seas. It was in their hearts to conquer Atlantis. They did not know that the existence of this island was remote and that it could stand as a fortress in itself. They wanted a kingdom of their own with mild climates to provide a bounty of food available at all times. With no worries of a supply of food they could put their energies into a life of engaging in a way of ruling that would give them full control over all. They had heard of the land of warmth and plenty in Atlantis and wanted to investigate for themselves.*

*These warriors took boats and headed straight toward this new land, Atlantis. They were not disappointed with what they saw. The first look at the island gave them the satisfaction that they could not only occupy a land of plenty but could easily set themselves up to be protected from intruders. This was a land of all lands that had the climate they desired as well as existing in a way that they would never fear intruders from the outside world. Soon they returned to their homeland to gather up their families to take them to Atlantis.*

*These warriors had many Gods existing in their minds. They did not believe that one God centered his mind on the needs of all and were determined to set up their own empire in their own way. There would be many Gods to worship.*

*They found it to be easy to live like kings on Atlantis. They had brought along those that they could control for their own use. It was slave labor that built the structures that you see below on the center of the island. Stone was plentiful and easy to obtain. The resulting castle is a magnificent structure of earthen stone. The castle was made in a way that it could be defended from any intruders.*

## ATLANTIS *A New View*

*The merchants who traveled the seas knew of the island of Atlantis. As the warriors established their kingdom, they also encouraged trade from afar. The mild climate and the abundance of food gave them the desired trading power. It wasn't long that merchant vessels were coming from the Atlantic side to Atlantis and left by the Red Sea. It was of no wonder that many traded in such a space of plenty. Merchants came from as far away as the Bearing Sea to what we know as the Atlantic Ocean to find these islands. They would leave to find the Red Sea and continue into other trading ports. Others came from other parts to trade. Atlantis grew and the kingdom became rich in trade.*

*Trading was pure power for this kingdom. Trade also brought others from other parts that were equally anxious to make their mark that could be in control of the lives of others. Greed breeds evil and so it too came to Atlantis."*

"**Kaluba abruptly stood up as he said,**" *"We shall continue this conversation another time. The light of day is fast leaving us and we have to walk a good way yet before we reach the top. There is a small village that we shall be passing through before we reach the top. If darkness comes upon us we can spend the night there. It is dangerous to be out on the trail after darkness."*

"**The group quickly got in line to follow Kaluba up the trail. It had been a refreshing and enjoyable stop. They wanted to hear the rest of the story but were in agreement that this would be no place to be if it got dark. Richa was nervous and hurried along. As she did so she watched her steps more closely so as not to stumble on the rocks in the path. She spotted a small blue stone and picked it up thinking it would make a great necklace.**

**Just as Kaluba had told them, they soon came upon a small village that had clay huts that were literally**

plastered to the side of the mountain. Children ran out to greet them. As the children darted in and out among the little group, they all made their way into the center of the village.

It was amazing that the villagers seemed to know they would be coming along shortly and had prepared a feast for their coming. It would be a different kind of feast than the group could have ever expected. They relished the thought of spending the night where it was safe and at the same time learn more about the people of Atlantis."

The Priests' mountain sanctuary, the perfect place to establish and grow the Atlantian way of life, and reach out to others.

# CHAPTER V:

## PRIESTS ON THE MOUNTAIN

Unique and I had been sitting in the garden for a very long time. She stood up and motioned for me to do the same. I thought this meant she intended to end her story of Atlantis for the night. It was not so; after a few minutes of stretching Unique sat back down and indicated I should do the same. I could see that she had no intention of ending her story for the evening as she continued, **"Kaluba, the priest led the way directly to the gathering place of all the villagers. It was dusk, but the three, Richa, Mikus and Federico could see the smiling faces of the hosts against the light from the fire and felt the warmth that the others projected in their greetings.**

**The setting was so different than the market place. There were men, women and children of all ages present. They were all dressed in cottons of various dark colors. It was so unlike the people at the market place where one saw many dressed in colorful silks. I wondered, was it from rich to the poor? I watched closely through Richa's eyes and waited for her thoughts to come to me.**

**As usual Richa did not miss seeing anything that was going on around her. As the villagers greeted her, she could see out of the corner of her eye that Kaluba was disappearing into one of the nearby cave like huts. She was comfortable in his presence and hoped he would return soon. The villagers understood that they were exhausted from the walk up the mountain and offered them clay cups of fresh water to drink along with giving each a basin of warm water to freshen up.**

Richa was just finishing washing her face when she saw that not one but many priests were walking toward the group of villagers. They all moved quickly to the fire where the villagers were standing and sat on the ground. The villagers took direction from the priests and followed suit and they also sat down on the ground. Richa quickly returned to the fire, as did Mikus and Federico. They too sat on the ground like the others. They knew from the priest's habits that they were positioning themselves for meditation. Everyone got very quiet including the children. Some bowed their heads and some looked up to the skies. There were others that were pulling strings of beads through their fingers. It appeared the group was respectful of the priests but took different methods in the way they would meditate.

After a long silence, Kaluba began chanting in a strange dialog, as did most of the others. I watched as Mikus and Federico joined in the chant but Richa remained silent. She did not seem to understand the chanting and so, therefore, I did not either. Not understanding did not seem to bother her though as she gave thanks in her own way. I could hear her thoughts as she thanked God for allowing her to be in the presence of the priests and the villagers.

Food was the next order and it was Kaluba that decided when it was time to eat. He arose and moved quickly to the area where the food had been set out. The priests that had joined Kaluba greeted the new comers as they too filed by toward the food. It all seemed so ritualistic. The foods they ate that night were breads made of grains. The priests called these humble foods. The only exotic foods served were heaps of unusual fresh fruits. There were mangos, bananas, and different kinds of berries that had no doubt been gathered in the jungle areas around the village.

    After the meal, the villagers quietly began to disburse with their children to the cave like huts for the night. Richa was asked to join some women in one of the huts and Mikus and Federico followed Kaluba and the other priests.

    They all slept on mats on the floor but having a shelter overhead seemed wonderful to Richa. This was the first time she had protection from the elements since leaving home. It rained heavily during the night as it did almost every night on Atlantis. The rest was refreshing and Richa was up early the next morning but no earlier than the priests and the villagers. The priests had already gathered in meditation as the women worked around an outdoor fire baking bread made from the grains. As the smell of baking bread rose into the air, the hosts heaped up a mound of fresh fruit into a huge clay bowl. This seemed to be the signal that the food was ready to eat and everyone gathered in one huge circle. There was meditation and then chanting just like the night before and then they filed to the bread and fruit. Richa and the others followed along as if they had done this every day of their lives.

    After eating, Richa wanted to talk further with the villagers as did Mikus and Federico. Talking would have to come at another time, as Kaluba and the other priests were ready to set out on the trail.

    The group fell in line with Kaluba taking the lead. To Richa's surprise the path leaving the village was on flat ground. The village sat on the edge of a large plateau that had been cleared of jungle growth. The villagers were using this open land to grow grains and vegetables.

After a short distance the group took another turn and the path became steep as it wound up the mountain. The jungle growth was now heavy on both sides of the path.

After climbing steadily upward for some time, the path opened out onto a long and narrow plateau. Next to the mountain side of the plateau were many clay huts. The huts were built crudely but one could see that they provided warmth for the priests that amassed here. Instead of children greeting them, this plateau area was full of monkeys. They were very noisy, as if they were scolding each other. As the group passed by the monkeys, Richa could see the remnants of fresh fruit along the path, near what seemed to be a feeding area. She would learn later that the monkeys were considered sacred to the priests and symbolized the good, in a spiritual way.

As the group approached the huts in the compound, many more priests appeared. They were dressed in long robes. Richa knew when she saw all of the priests, that they had finally reached their destination. She welcomed the sight.

The priests greeted Richa, Mikus and Federico warmly. It was Richa though that brought a stunned look to their faces when they greeted her. She felt it was because she was a woman and was dressed as a priest. If the priests knew everything as Kaluba had said, they obviously had not been told that there was going to be a woman among them.

Kaluba directed Richa to a small hut on the edge of a ledge that was not far from the placement of the other huts. She was told this was to be her quarters. Kaluba showed her where the water was for drinking and pointed to a mat rolled up on the floor to be a place for

## RICHA'S PLAN

resting and meditating. Without further words Kaluba left her there and joined the others. Richa feared that she was being ostracized from the group, but it was only a short time and Kaluba returned for her. He took her to another hut where the priests were amassed. She realized on entering, from the somber looks, that the priests had been discussing her presence there. Kaluba was intent on resolving any issue head on by having Richa speak for herself.

Richa knew from what she had been told that if one wanted to become a priest, it could take an entire lifetime to pass the steps required. Even if she had this kind of wish, she could not be certain, as a woman, that she would be able to attain the priesthood. The last step to becoming a priest required great strength and only the males were looked at as having this capability.

Priests were required to complete different steps, or as they called them, paths before their final enlightenment. Richa knew well the path of meditation and seeing. All her life she had used meditation to find the peace that allowed her to see visions. She knew the kindness that she needed to portray to be in light with God's ways. Now she was being asked to speak in her own behalf as to why she had chosen to come to Atlantis.

As my thoughts followed Richa, I could literally hear the wheels of her mind turning. Richa was quick witted in how she could gain the confidence of others. She had been told that the priests worked day and night to help those on the island that had strayed into evil ways. She knew the priests were weary at how many souls had gotten caught up and lost forever in a time of evil. She also knew that the priests were relentless in their cause and needed all the help they could find to seek out and help these lost souls.

It was with these thoughts that she stood before the priests and proclaimed her part in the cause to help others. There was determination in her voice as she told them she would be presenting herself as a messenger, not as a priestess. In this way, she would follow the way of the priests in how she set about helping others. It was in that way that they listened and agreed to allow her to study their paths and to walk in the way of destroying evil.

It was amazing how Richa turned the tide from resentment to acceptance among the priests. I knew by now that there were many strengths within this young lady's methods, but I would find in the days ahead that there were many more sides of her wisdom that I had not seen.

Richa had been formulating a plan as she walked up the mountain, and now she set about to put it into action. The first step in her plan would be to learn as much about the priests as she could. She knew they liked to tell stories and if they believed that she was sincere, they would be teaching her to follow their ways and they would be more than willing to enlighten her.

She felt that Kaluba was not distraught by all her questions and would be willing to help her. It was easy for her to determine Kaluba's pattern in life and to find the right time to seek him out. The middle of the afternoon, after he arose from resting and meditation, was just the right time. Richa had many questions about the priests and Atlantis.

Richa was right in seeing Kaluba as the right teacher. Every afternoon she found Kaluba sitting in the same quiet place.  She would join him and proceed to ask him questions.  After the first few days, these conversations with Kaluba became a daily ritual.  It was not long before Mikus and Federico also joined them.  Having a group to teach, pleased Kaluba.  The other priests joined the group from time to time, but never interfered with Kaluba in any way.

Kaluba listened to Richa's many questions and was amused at her persistence, but was always kind in answering.  I wondered if Richa was considering the challenges of becoming a priestess, but I reminded myself that questions were a natural pattern for her.

It is easier to tell my story when Kaluba tells you in his own words as he told the little group.  He first spoke of the priests' desire to come to Atlantis.  This is what he said, "The priests that you see here today were amassed on a small island outside the circle of Atlantis.  We had come to this island from a large mass of land a great distance from here by boats. We found that there was plenty of food and the climate was warm on our new island.  We were the only occupants of this island and we were happy here but not fulfilled.  Our vows, as priests, are sacred to us and we needed to share our gifts with others.

We heard of Atlantis from the merchants that stopped by our island from time to time.  We knew from the merchants that there was a mass destruction of souls going on at Atlantis that did not follow the rule of our own beliefs.  We knew from our prayers and visions that we must go to Atlantis and find ways that would allow the souls involved in this evil to heal.

It was with this in mind that we came to Atlantis.  We came by boat and arrived in a mass.  The market was full of merchants and locals trading goods. We were looked at as intruders because we were priests. The rulers did not fear us but avoided us. The others were respectful, but wary of becoming too friendly and thus antagonizing the rulers. It was not comfortable for us to remain at the market place where the activity was not conducive to our way of life. We needed a quiet place where we could find our own peace. This mountain sanctuary that we reside was just the right place for our priests to establish our way of life and to reach out to others.

After we settled into our own daily routine, we made plans to help others. We knew it was not good for the evil that existed here on Atlantis. They were taking the minds of man and inserting them into animals of a certain breed. We knew they must be stopped from trying to create a new breed of man. We knew from God's own words that many could be delivered from such times. It would be our task to heed those warnings and help those that could be touched by God. They must change their own ways and stop ruling in such a savage way over all.

The makeshift caves that we have here provided the warmth for our priests. Here we could be safe and not directly interfere with the rulers. We were close enough to shed some light about God and to develop the plans to help as many as we could. It was God that we listened to and allowed him to guide us.

It was easy to move among the others on Atlantis and be recognized as priests. Our robes were brown as you see them now. We portrayed a simple life. The rulers of evil set themselves apart by wearing silks of many colors. The silks flowed in the air as they walked. They felt then as they do now, that this dress gave them an air of superiority over others. As you saw in the market place, the colors are beautiful pastels that are made from flower petal dyes. The fabrics have been woven from many places and arrived at Atlantis harbors where the evils snatched them up.

We priests are followers of God and use prayer to answer our causes. We knew that this island would one day be destroyed. It is a daily struggle to find those lost souls and to allow them to find the need of God's own ways.

We give thanks to the stars that show us the light and that keeps us together in a mass, so as not to be destroyed by the evil minds that are here. It is our own power and our strength in our beliefs that does not allow them to persuade us to change.

God has given us visions that tell us of the evil actions that will be destroyed along with the island. He has told us that we will be led to safe ground and will not be destroyed. Knowing that it will be only a matter of time before we are led from this place we have much work to accomplish here in a short time. It is our challenge to help others. It is in this challenge that we look to all three of you, Richa, Mikus and Federico to help us.

Through our many visions came thoughts that were clear to us on how to proceed. We aligned our thoughts in a way that allowed us to know that the love we created in sharing God's ways helped others find more love. They in turn share in the love of others. We are priests that rise up in ways that will allow our followers to change their ways. In our inspirations that we share, we can help fill in the voids of destruction that they have seen here.

# ATLANTIS *A New View*

    In your own messages to the people, you will use the same methods that we are using to help others. You may share the same stories that we have shared with you by passing them on to others. The stories will enlighten others so they too will want to share.
    As a priest I work with other priests that have followed our beliefs. We believe that God is the center of all universes and is the protector of all souls that come along. We know that it is not in the best interest of the people to follow those that do not love in God's own ways. We know, as priests, that we must link together to provide the means to reach out and allow them the desires to follow God's ways.
    We are warriors of a different kind. Not in taking up the same arms as a warrior, but using our methods to go from soul to soul to try to uplift them in the way that God intended for them to know. We do not destroy those that have chosen evil, but we lead those that are willing to find their own way without evil ways.
    There is a reason that I am telling you all of this. You have offered to help us with our work here. Your ways are perhaps somewhat different in the way you progress, but not in the end results.
    I can tell that you Richa, have your own plan and your own way. Knowing this only tells me that we can also learn from you as you follow God's path. You Mikus and Federico have spoken of your own desires to be priests in our way and therefore will join us in studying the paths that we follow. Our ways will become your own in time.
    There are smart and dumb and rich and poor that circulates this island. There are those that are religious and not so religious. There are those that will take on

other souls to fight their way through. I know that you Richa, are eager to help and want to find those souls that need to find a clearer vision. You have said you know that you have made the right choice to come here. I know you are eager to meet up with many that have lost their own control and will work to help them find the light to carry on. I will assist you in these ways."

Richa, Mikus and Federico were happy to be accepted into the lives of the priests. They knew that they would be guided in ways that would be helpful, but they also knew that the priests expected results.

In the days ahead, Kaluba told them stories of enlightenment. The three would use these same stories to share with others. The stories were of those souls that had found enlightenment. The priests would visit villages to find villagers that would approach them. In this way those that seemed to be at the waters edge of self destruction had someone to help them.

To help them in their quest, the priests used prayers. They had many dreams in which God came to them. They shared with others and told of the dreams that God gave them that answered their prayers.

They spoke of evil when the priests intervened, but there were other causes that brought the priests to help others. When someone was sick and needed a hand to help them through, they were there with prayers.

The priests shared stories of heroics that saved others that did not know the true meaning of God's power. It was stories of love that were shared with those that had chosen the wrong roads.

There were many stories that Kaluba shared with Richa, Mikus and Federico in their afternoon sessions about the rulers and the evil of Atlantis. I will share all of this with you, but first I want to tell you about Richa and the others during the mornings. Richa used this free time to pursue her own plan. Mikus and Federico joined her, as did Kaluba on many occasions.

    Richa was absorbing all that Kaluba told them but she was also anxious to learn of the island on her own. Her free mornings left her time to explore. Mikus and Federico were happy to join her on her explorations. They knew that Richa had her own gifts of wisdom and wanted to be in on her plan. From experience, they knew that she too could look deeper into those souls that were careless in their ways and could offer them enlightenment that they could not refuse."

# CHAPTER VI:

## RICHA'S PLAN

My friend, Unique stopped talking for a moment as if to catch her breath. The moon was high in the sky and the night air had cooled the garden. It was getting late but I knew from watching Unique that she was not ready to stop for the evening. I quickly poured her some hot coffee from a thermos.

As Unique sipped her drink she said, **"To understand Richa is to understand myself. It is as if I am looking into a mirror at my own soul. It is a very strange feeling, but it has proven to be a great enlightenment to me. First, finding that I could indeed visit my past at my calling has been a marvel in itself. Then to find that I could follow the path of my own soul within the life of Richa's has been amazing. The greatest inspiration of all is in telling Richa's story and knowing that you will share it with others. In this way, others will have an awareness of new possibilities. Anyone with the desire can then use their own methods, or the ones I use, to find the calmness that can take the mind within. This allows anyone to find their own answers from their own souls.**

As I pieced Richa's story together, from the many visits to my past, I found that her plan to help others on Atlantis was parallel to my own life on earth. I don't mean in the day to day things, but in the paths that I have chosen today. Richa was as determined as I can be when I set goals and so it is as we will follow her through the next days on Atlantis.

Richa felt her path was predetermined by the many visions she had. She saw that she could weld the minds with thoughts around the individual's own interests. In this way, each could use their own interests to expose the atrocities of the evil that came their way.

She felt that she was guided by her visions to proceed with her own plan. She had visions about those around her, so she knew that they would come together and be part of her plan. There were also visions of plans that could be controlled. She determined that sharing those visions would justify the awareness that was meant to be. It must become a goal to reach out to others. In reaching out to others they could find a pattern and then destroy the evil that had been inflicted over them. In this way, they would all be led on to believe in God.

When Richa told Mikus and Federico of her visions and her plan, they were interested but skeptical of her ability to make it work. The priests had questioned her ability as a priestess because she was a woman and the villagers might do the same.

This revelation from her two loyal friends only fired up Richa's determination to not let any skeptical views get in her way. Thinking of what Mikus and Federico said enabled her to turn her charm on them as if they were the villagers. Her friends already knew from experience that her gifts were like magic and she could convince others that they could believe in her words. She felt they were skeptics more because she was a woman than because of the words she could speak. Richa asked for guidance through prayer and the answer she received was clear. Both Mikus and Federico were ready to bring their own desires into focus. How better to do that than to help them reach into their own souls for answers to questions that they needed to find and then deliver them to others. Their stories with Richa's stories would then become a combination of revelations and no one would consider if they came from man or woman.

Richa determined that all the stories, including those from the other priests, would make up the total plan that each would present to convince the villagers of God's ways. Their stories would be of miracles from their own visions and also of times long ago. The stories would set the pattern to find a better goal.

Both Mikus and Federico desired to become priests. In their own right they had found the calmness needed to proceed with thoughts to the soul. Both men could find their own visions that added to the stories they already had.

Richa proceeded with her plan by spending time each morning to set with her friends. They each meditated in their own way and shared what they saw. The enlightenment that Richa shared with them gave them confidence in knowing that their own visions would increase over time.

Richa's plan did not end there. She knew that Mikus and Federico would be accompanying her to the villages in the mornings, so she decided that Kaluba should join them, if he was willing. His presence would insure the villagers of their sincerity. After all, this new friend had his own desire to protect the villagers from evil. Having three more following his own path pleased him and he readily joined the little group.

There were daily treks to the surrounding villages. The villages were hidden from view, but Kaluba knew all the trails to find them. The village sites were located on the side of the mountain not far from each other. The villagers always greeted them warmly, but with hesitation, until they saw Kaluba was one of the group.

ATLANTIS *A New View*

His presence instantly comforted them. He had visited them many times and they knew they could trust him to not bring them any harm.

And so the daily routine began with Kaluba leading the way to the villages. As the villagers gathered around, it became story time. Richa wanted to be looked at as a messenger rather than a priestess, so she always began with what she knew of marvels from long ago.

I listened in on her thoughts through my own soul and knew that the stories of the ancients in Italy would be the first she told. I learned from her that the ancients were people who ruled in an earlier time. Their core of existence was to relay the love that God had for them. Richa's stories were good to know, but as a wise storyteller she always shed new light on the stories that paralleled a meaning for the present times on Atlantis. She mixed her stories with the visions she had from God, knowing that they would display a need for love for all.

There was no resistance to her stories with the villagers because she was a woman. They listened to her with the same exuberance that Kaluba, Mikus and Federico got from their stories. As the days passed, it was obvious that the stories had taken on a life of their own and each of the four began to borrow enlightenment from the others, so that they could share it with the villagers. There was a great pleasure in traveling together from village to village, but there was a bigger need tugging at Richa that she had yet to develop.

One morning the group was visiting a village on the far side of the mountain from the market place. The village had the most tranquil setting. There was a magnificent view of the open seas stretching away from the island. Richa looked down at the side of the

# RICHA'S PLAN

mountain to the water's edge below and could see white sand on the beach stretching out in both directions.

Kaluba saw the longing to investigate in Richa's eyes and suggested that they take a path to the beach. Richa was delighted to have the opportunity to walk to the beach. The others were willing to take a break from their daily story telling. The small group wound their way down the path. They again were told to be careful of the yellow and black snakes that dwelled in this area near the seashore. The path was narrow with heavy growth of trees and grasses on either side. There were beautiful clusters of yellow and gold flowers that nestled in clumps among the bushes. The flowers were radiant. She had not realized that the trees could have such a growth, yet they mingled well with the other bushes where the flowers grew in large masses.

As they walked close to the bushes, the insects around the flowers were disturbed. Richa could see them against the light of the sky flying here and there. She did not appreciate them flying around her head, but realized it was the nectar of the flowers that they were after.

Her inspirational juices had begun to flow when she spotted the many clumps of flowers. She knew that these beautiful yellow and gold petals would be excellent to make a dye with for the creations she could make from clay.

She also knew that the villagers gathered clay from the sides of the streams that dumped water into the ocean. The clay would be perfect to use with the dye from the yellow flowers. In her mind, she planned to gather clay from along the banks of the streams and take it back up the mountain to work her own wonders with.

# ATLANTIS *A New View*

    Richa was tempted to stop and pick some of the yellow and gold flowers, but her thoughts reminded her of the snakes. She would remember where the flowers were and return to the same spot when she had time to get help from the others to thrash the bushes and scare any snakes into retreat.
    Soon the path opened out onto the beach. The sun was rising in the sky with lights bouncing off of the glistening sand. The others were intent on the view of the ocean, but Richa could not take her eyes from the glistening on the sandy beach. As she got closer, she could see that the beach was strewn with the most beautiful blue stones. She picked one up and instantly recognized its color as being exactly like the one she had found on the path that they had traveled weeks ago from the market place. The blue stones brought another artistic idea to Richa's mind. The blue stones, the clay, and the flower petal dye would all be her canvas. Creations from these finds would be the tools to move the mind to the soul to find messages from God. She would present her gifts to the villagers to inspire them.
    Mikus and Federico knew of Richa's talents from the creations she made at home in Italy. They knew how she was able to inspire others from her art work that became her tool to help others believe in God. They were enthusiastic to help her gather the stones of all sizes.
    They all began to gather the stones of blue. Among the blue stones, they saw small agate rocks with flat surfaces on the beach and gathered them also. They were exuberant in their find and were quickly beginning to fill the goat skin sacks that they carried.
    It was Federico who first spotted the clay that he knew Richa would want for her work. He helped her collect

# RICHA'S PLAN

the clay in a large goat's bag and then packed the top with moist moss to keep it from drying out.

It was late afternoon when they returned to the priest's quarters on the mountain, but all were pleased at what had transpired that day. Richa was surprised to see that Federico had packed some yellow flowers on top of the packs of clay. His thoughtfulness made it possible for Richa's plan to be complete. The story telling would continue but she would squeeze in time to work on her creations.

The days flew by as the group continued their daily trips to the villages. In spite of Richa insisting that she was only a messenger, the villagers spoke of her as a priestess with many stories. She shared in this admiration with her friends, Kaluba, Mikus and Federico. The other priests on the mountain were also pleased at the work done by the four who traveled to the villages. They did whatever they could to help the villagers discover love and kindness in knowing God.

Richa set about gathering more flowers besides the beautiful yellow and gold specimens that she had found. There were purple and white flowers and a host of different colored leaves. Often she used the flower petal colors separately for dye colors. Other times she blended them together to melt as one to change the colors of her dyes.

One of her favorite colors was the deep yellow flower petal dye that she added to her clay and then molded it into small round shapes. She used tiny twigs to make small holes in the center of the pebble. She then threw the clay rounds into pots and allowed them to heat on the fires. When she finished this process, she would remove the pebbles that were still hot and shine them with huge leaves from the many plants that surrounded her quarters.

The sheen that the leaves gave the stones controlled the color to different intensities. After she polished the stones, she put them into clay pots to be heated and then again polished them with green leaves. The finished product was a bead of sorts and it shimmered in its own beauty. She used the beads for others to look at and use to control their present times. These were special gifts of beads to transform their minds into their own spirituality. She presented them to the villagers with love.

The monkeys in the compound where Richa lived with the priests were mischievous. The monkeys were attracted to the bright colors of her creations. They especially liked the yellow clay beads. Some days when she was heating the rounds in pots, it was a race between Richa and the monkeys to see who got to the hot stones first. The monkeys thought the yellow beads were there to be eaten. One by one they discovered the stone were hot to the touch and would scamper away only to come back another time and try again to help themselves.

Richa solved most of the monkey theft by waiting for the feeding time of the monkeys at their own feeding station. The monkeys had learned that the priests were very timely in this process and watched for them daily.

The flat agate stones that Richa and her friends gathered along the beach also became a canvas. She used the dyes she had created from the flower petals to make drawings. She dipped feathers into the dye and allowed her mind to create. These finished pictures became symbols that she said represented the presence of God in their lives. To have one of these creations was a special gift the villagers treasured because it was from their favorite priestess.

She also used flowers to make arrangements along with the islands best plants to display with the flowers. She mixed the colors carefully to represent colors that influenced the feeling of love. Her art was beautiful and it instilled the love in others when they knew it was the beauty that surrounded them. It filled their minds with peace and that evoked a special kindness. It helped them learn the difference between finding God's love and knowing that the evil that was around them could destroy them.

The blue stones that Richa and the others had collected were truly amazing. She discovered that the stones would change colors in the light to respond to the environment around them. The colors would radiate in different ways. The hues were of blue, but they adjusted to other colors when viewed in different lights. The stones could magnify the distance with their own wonders. She knew these stones were another of God's miracles to help put visions into symbols to reveal the power of God's love. She knew if those that came her way could take the stones in their hand, the brilliance would penetrate their minds in a way to know God had touched them and they would believe. It was another way of establishing a bond with God. Richa simply devised ways for others to see the beautiful stones in the same way that she saw them.

She remembered that the ancients of Italy had used similar stones to see into their own visions and that would light their way. They used the stones as crystals of the sky. The sky would illuminate from the heavens and they could see into great distances when the light was reflected from the stones. The ancients of Italy found many uses from similar stones.

Richa saw visions from the carved pendants and that became more symbols for her. She looked upon them as ways to help the villagers grow and learn of God when they were sincere in his ways. The symbols themselves were an expression to be dealt with through the mind. The images expressed love and courage and kindness that were for all to find through the divine. The idea was to spread the thoughts into the symbols and then express those ideas to the villagers to make it clearer for them to know about God.

From her visions, Richa made medallions of light that represented symbols of messages from God. If the villagers were to find their own souls, they must first discover a method to see deep within. The medallions of light represented God's own love for them to find better times. Those that came Richa's way would take the medallions of light into their own hands and see the visions appear before their own eyes. They were not actually seeing visions, but believed by the brilliance and warmth and color of the stones that God's presence had touched them. They were then willing to follow Richa's words to find their own wisdom.

If they saw a vision of an angel in the warmth of the stone, it would allow them the thoughts of God's own presence and they would adjust their own ways to see into their own souls. They thought of Richa as a priestess and a messenger of God. The stones only allowed their own thoughts to expand on her messages, but when they believed, many miracles could be achieved. Her goal was to spread love and kindness from within.

# RICHA'S PLAN

When I think of Richa's methods, I find myself meditating more under the stars and that gives me peace. It must be similar to those times that she looked at the stones and lovingly handed them to the others for their own peace.

Richa was learning the ways of the priests and of the villagers on Atlantis. Time was passing and she had not heard directly from Kaluba as to what to expect by the deformities that occurred from the evil that existed on the beautiful island.

Richa had wondered for weeks why Kaluba was reluctant to talk about the evil on the island. She snuffed her impulses to ask him any questions, knowing that he would decide on his own timing when to tell her. He must have thought Richa was ready to hear the worst of the atrocities when he invited Richa to join him one afternoon in what he called a council between all of the priests."

ATLANTIS *A New View*

# CHAPTER VII:

## EVILS OF ATLANTIS

Unique continued telling her story, "I could hear Richa's thoughts vibrating in my mind as Kaluba asked her to join the other priests in council. She was afraid they were going to ask her to find quarters somewhere else. She felt that she had disrupted the quiet of the compound because the monkeys kept invading her space in search of her bright yellow beads. She was sorry for that, but had not found any other way to quiet the monkeys, except to fire the beads of clay when the priests fed the monkeys.

The priests were already seated on mats when Richa entered the hut with Kaluba. He motioned for her to be seated at the right of Mikus and Federico. Kaluba sat on a mat near the center of the group. Immediately everyone became quiet and Kaluba led a prayer. As it was at other times, Richa did not understand the chanting, but gave her own prayers in the same way that she had done before.

The chanting seemed to last longer than usual, but when it finally stopped, Richa sat quietly and stiffly in anticipation of what might come. Kaluba stood up and to her amazement asked her to stand also. He spoke in a firm voice with a slight smile on his face. In one hand was a large goat skin bag and he gestured Richa to take it and pass the contents around so that the others could see.

She recognized the bag as the one she had given Kaluba to hold samples of each of her creations. She saw that the bag still contained her own creations. There were yellow and gold beads of clay, agate rocks with symbols drawn on them and beautiful blue stones with carved symbols. As Richa passed out the creations to the priests to examine, their stony faces turned to smiles. Did the smiles mean that they liked her works of art? She thought that at the least she might be able to defend her presence among them by sharing how her creations had touched the villagers.

Richa sat back down on her mat as Kaluba began speaking to the group. As he spoke, the other priests were still passing the different art works among themselves. She was relieved when she heard Kaluba explain that each art piece was a wonder of its own. He told them that holding or wearing these gifts of art helped the villagers find the calm they needed to find God's ways.

Richa was surprised when Kaluba held up a string of yellow beads. He had strung the individual beads on a very small vine. She recognized the vine as growing profusely nearby. She had made holes in the beads for stringing, but had decided against it because the beads went further when she distributed them one by one among the villagers.

Kaluba proclaimed to the rest that when he passed the beads through his fingers, it brought a peaceful calm to his mind. After having said that, Kaluba turned to other matters that were in all their minds. He spoke of the new people that continued to flow to the island from far away places. They took up roots in an oasis of wonder, only to find there was evil among the good.

Kaluba opened the discussion to the other priests and they spoke of what they were seeing. They were all alarmed at the way villagers continued to disappear to never be seen again. The priests felt that their work was good, but it was not enough to keep the villagers from being taken one by one. The evil ones would perform their hideous acts on them in the laboratories.

Richa knew by now that the evil ones used animal parts to implant into the bodies of their victims, the villagers. Exotic animals that did not exist on Atlantis were brought in by the merchants from other parts of the world for their experiments. She knew the intent was for the humans to take on the traits of the animals that were implanted in them. She was disgusted at the thought, but had not seen the laboratories at work, except from a distance. In fact, she had not seen the deformed villagers that had gone through the laboratory experiments. She had been told about them, but for the most part, they stayed out of the view of others.

Richa felt the same anguish that the priests had felt. All of them had experienced the grief of the villagers when a member had been taken.

She had been so intent on what the others were saying that she did not realize Kaluba had approached her mat. He told her that the council was about to begin their group studies for the priesthood and this would be a good time for her to leave before they began. It was with great relief that she returned to her own quarters, knowing now that they were not going to ask her to live somewhere else.

Later that morning many of the priests came by to pick up a handful of the bright yellow beads. Richa was pleased, as she knew they would string them in the same way that Kaluba had and use them for calming the mind.

It was that same day, in the afternoon, that Kaluba met with Richa, Mikus and Federico and he began telling them more of the details of the evils of Atlantis. He spoke

# ATLANTIS *A New View*

of their first presence on Atlantis when they appeared from another land. He described how they set up the laboratories and he shared their purpose behind their plan. As Kaluba continued his story, he took them to another setting on the island, so that they could view the center of the evil that was bringing down the villagers. It was Kaluba's intent for them to know the details, so that they could become even more effective in helping the villagers escape such tragic ends.

Over the days ahead, Kaluba told his story."

*"The people of evil came to Atlantis from Egypt. They came from a culture that demanded them to fall into line and to obey those that had set them up. It was a group that had their own passions and they wanted to portray those goals. They knew of Atlantis' beauty with its land of plenty. They also knew that the people of Atlantis were ruled by a powerful king. They also knew the king was a ruler of great power among the villagers and he could be controlled with gifts to support his own pleasures.*

*In coming to Atlantis, they felt they could incorporate their own desires into a plan that would give them the power to rule the whole earth. The island would provide plenty of food and opportunities for enjoyment along the way. They would experiment with man and animal to eliminate the weakest breed and produce only those breeds that would destruct on their commands.*

*These men looked at God as only a myth. They planned to be creative in a destructive way so as not to produce any love. In this way the power of free will would be obliterated.*

*The evil men were swarthy looking and rugged. They relied on using their minds that they felt were superior, to create a mind that would follow them. They were only interested in their own passions. It was in their minds to create a leadership over all others and to take control of those around them. These acts would set them apart from all others with a belief that they would then become the rulers of the world.*

*These evil men were an intelligent group with scientific minds. They had studied the process of thoughts between others to find answers. They came with knowing about the transportation of thoughts from space and how that could work in their own favor to develop a desired path. They knew well of the human body and all of its needs. It was incorporating what they had learned and studied in their own home land that would allow them to develop a masterful plan to control other minds.*

*Their plan included using animals like lions and tigers for the strength of their muscles and quickness of their minds. They would create a different kind of man. In time, they would control a race that would not be inhibited, but would grow in ways only to glorify them.*

*In their laboratories, they set about using their abilities to surgically implant body parts of animals into humans to develop another culture. In pairing up the analysis, they decided it was time to experiment on humans and animals in yet a different way.*

*Their intent was not to destroy the minds of those existing. They would capitalize on that existence for the cells to formulate a pro existence with others. They wanted a new culture and were not satisfied to develop a method that would help mankind, but would destroy those that were living to develop a man that could not be conquered.*

*They analyzed the cells to find the traits that would work well together. From conquering and dividing the right cell implants, they developed a uniqueness to see into their own visions. Their process was rigid and many experiments ended up on the lab floor. They still proceeded to find the right methods that would alter man forever."*

"During one of his stories of the evil, Kaluba suggested that they view the laboratories from a closer vantage point. Richa, Mikus, Federico and Kaluba were about to set off down the mountain when several other priests joined them. Kaluba nodded to them as if it was preplanned that they would be going with them.

In an explanation, Kaluba told the group that it was safer if they traveled together in a larger group. Richa thought they were going to a spot above the market place, but half way down the mountain Kaluba took a side trail that that took them to a vantage point above the water below. They walked over the rough rock terrain that soon leveled out to a rocky ledge where they could look straight down to the water. The priests seemed to know exactly where they were headed and the only surprised ones were Richa, Mikus and Federico. They came to a spot along the ledge that was overgrown with vines and other grown vegetation. Right in the middle of the vegetation was a large stream that tumbled down the mountain and over the rocky edge.

Kaluba stopped just at the edge of the stream and made a quick turn into the bushes along the edge of the cliff where they would all be hidden from view. Just below, next to the water, were the laboratories. They recognized them as the laboratories that Kaluba had pointed out the first time they met him on the trail going up from the market place. The buildings of the laboratories were made of stone and they were built along a ledge that went straight down to the water edge below.

# EVILS OF ATLANTIS

The group was perfectly concealed by the growth and had a birds eye view of all that lay below them. They could even see the brown stone castle further on around the edge of the water. It was here that Kaluba told the rest of his story.

We gathered close to Kaluba so that we could hear his voice above the tumbling water. His voice was strong and clear as he continued his story."

*"You can see from the castle that there is a king on Atlantis. From the beginning, Atlantis arose from the sea from many rumblings of the earth and the vegetation began to grow. As the charm of Atlantis became known, so did its popularity for a place of paradise to live. As the stories go, Atlantis has always had a king in control. Control was passed down from one king to another. There are many Greek myths about the first king being a descendent of the Greek God Posidien. I can not deny that or verify it. As a priest from a faraway land, I came with my own convictions but I also came with an open mind.*

*We know now that the present king is controlling in his own way. He flaunts his power and wealth over others. You saw some of his kind dressed in silk robes in the market place. In a sense the king's men are members of the group of evil.*

*When the evil men came to Atlantis there was a chemistry reaction between the evil and the king. Both wanted power and both wanted to rule over others. It was easy for the evil to convince the king that he could retain his power and also be in on a greater plan to perform miracles of control in the new laboratories to be built on the island. The king agreed and gave them the use of his strongest men to build the laboratories that you see near the castle along the waters edge.*

*There was a purpose for building the laboratories along the waters edge. Many thought it was for the convenience of coming and going, but in reality it was to be near the water, so that they could dispose of the bodies that did not make the mold in the way that they planned.*

*As the laboratories were completed, the evil men set about with their plan to snare their prey. They had continued to think about ways that would control a race to only take orders from them. They would be the true victors and would rule all of those that came their way. They began to maneuver those capabilities in what they called scientific feats that would find the links for using animals to strengthen man.*

*They spread their own word and described God as having unjust ways. They told them that they would project the true meanings into what they could find to be man. They would deliver to the masses a new mental mask that would allow their minds to seek out new justices. The strength that could be found in incorporating such a veil to those that would submit, would allow them to spread their own powers into new ways. Those around them witness the heroics of what man could accomplish if they had the strength of animals. The new breed of man would collapse those outside forces and would ride high on the glories of having the strength and muscles that would abound.*

*The evil ones had no care of the human species. They only wanted to provide the world with a series of occupants that would control all of the ground and provide them with a safe haven to dwell on. They were not unique in their desires. They wanted to use their minds to create a power that would capitalize on thoughts to provide them well with the abilities of scientists.*

# EVILS OF ATLANTIS

*Their plan would allow them to control the ones that presently followed God's ways. They especially wanted those followers so that they could give a contrast to the others to see that those following God's ways would perish before all other kinds. They would not be helped by a God who could not see them. It was a display of power to be viewed by the wary, to convince them they could rule and be superior against any other kind if they trusted the experiments.*

*The evil men set up yet another plan as they canvassed the villages looking for the right men to begin their experiments with. Next to the laboratories was a compound that had another use.*

*The laboratories were well constructed and state of the art for that time. They used their scientific minds to create a laboratory paradise. The laboratories were even more immaculate than one could imagine, yet the work was so horrible that they became the mass grave for animals and mankind that did not link well in the experiments.*

*I shall mince no words, so that you will know that what happens here came from a plan for power and was turned into the mass destruction of mankind.*

*These evil men became deceitful breeds in retrospect. They used the compounds for parties fashioned for their enjoyment. To strengthen themselves, they had to be destructive so that they could control their victim's minds. At these parties they altered the victim's minds with drugs that destroyed the thought patterns when the liquid was drank.*

*To this day, they use the women for their own glories and liquor for their own desires to produce their own seeds that will make new cells for their own kinds.*

## ATLANTIS *A New View*

*The evil ones provide the villagers with food that is always plentiful. They have many feasts to entice the villagers to come. Lots of eating and drinking is encouraged. They provide lambs, fish and other animals. The growth on the island provides them with many nuts and berries. They concoct a batter from a course grain like substance that is as small as a mustard seed. This batter is formed into patties to be taken to the pots to cook for a long time. It is a specialty of the island and this bread like portion is secreted with juices from the fruits. When absorbed, it is like a glaze that can be eaten with more fruit. It melts in the mouth and one never tires of its richness.*

*This food is of a quality that the villagers can not resist but there is more to be told and it can be best said if we join the villagers at one of these feasts. Not all of the feasts are held at the compound you are viewing below. Come, we have just about enough daylight to reach the village compound above us before dusk takes us over."*

"We followed Kaluba up the trail the same way we had come, but then he veered off in another direction and on to another trail. The going was all up hill, but it was not long before our group broke out into an opening where we saw a village compound. This was a village that Richa had never visited.

The villagers greeted the priests as they did in all of the villages, except the arrival of priests always began the preparation for a feast. In this village the preparation for another kind of feast had already begun. Among those preparing the food were men dressed in silks that exposed many colors. Richa was frightened at first because of what she knew of the evil ones. Kaluba quieted her fears by assuring her that as priests in a group, these men would not harm them. They would have an eye out for the weaker villagers.

Richa discovered other villagers were arriving. They were coming just for the feast. They brought their own recipes and the feast became bigger as the crowds enlarged in size. It was not difficult to enjoy the festivities. Richa and the priests liked it when the food was presented and the crowd was having fun and enjoying the companionship among each other.

When the feasts continued on into the night, Richa and the others did not appreciate the evil charm of the festivities. The evil men brought out casks of liquid that they had fermented into a wine of their own choice. This liquid would only make them all crazy. Richa and the other priests melted into the background as the festivities got out of hand. There was no controlling what happened next.

The villagers were spread out over the ground in a stupor and the evil men in silk clothes, easily chose the ones they wanted to take to their laboratories. There was absolutely no resistance. If the priests were to speak out, it would only bring bloodshed from the evil ones.

It was with heavy hearts that Richa and the other priests took refuge in the huts with the villagers that had not drunk the mind controlling liquid. Kaluba told them they would be staying to help the villagers as they sobered up.

Richa felt that she was in the middle of what she knew was evil but she had no power to help the villagers drive off the evil men. She knelt on a mat as did the other priests and the villagers. Even the children joined them. Kaluba bowed in meditation and began to chant. The villagers in the hut followed Kaluba in chanting and Richa prayed in her own way.

It was a night that Richa would never forget. After praying for what seemed hours she realized that the compound was eerily quiet."

# EVILS OF ATLANTIS

The Laboratories could be seen in the distance.
Such horrible things were done there.
Test subjects, spent and expired, just thrown away.

ATLANTIS *A New View*

## CHAPTER VIII:

### EVIL VERSUS GOOD

"Richa had not slept that night, but neither had anyone else, except the children that had taken refuge in huts with them. Richa and the priests waited in the huts for daylight. As soon as there was morning light they left the hut to view the remains in the compound.

The evil men had departed and the large fire that had been burning brightly in the center of the compound existed as embers among the rocks. There were bodies strewn around on the ground as if they were pieces of wood. They were the men and the women that the evil ones had left behind. They were still in a deep stupor from the fermented liquid that they had drunk. They had been the lucky ones that were not chosen by the evil ones for the laboratory experiments.

As the priests stoked up the fire to see better, the villagers appeared from other huts. They dispersed quickly to search the compound for their family members. Richa could hear the anguished cries of the villagers calling out for the ones that were missing.

Instinctively Richa and the priests moved quickly among the villagers to soothe their cries. Some blamed the priests for not doing anything to save the missing loved ones. Others understood that a priest was bound by their beliefs to never become combative. The villagers that were among the believers knew that God allowed free will. Free will was at hand when the villagers chose to drink the fermented liquid. If they had used their free will to abstain they would still be with their families.

One by one the villagers that had come from other villages left with those that were able to travel. Richa and the priests remained at the village through out the day and the next night. They nursed the villagers that needed care into a more peaceful state with a liquid made from herbs that they brewed.

There was meditation and prayer for the villagers. Richa and the priests spent another night at the village. The next morning Richa and the priests joined the villagers again in meditation and prayer. It was a sad time for the group. They felt remorse in knowing they could not have done more. In the days past they had often preached to any villagers they met that it was God's will that would bring Atlantis down if all refused to heed his warnings. They told the villagers that it wasn't right to take animal parts and attach them to humans. This only destroys what God has given to all.

The group bid goodbye and set out down the trail. Kaluba was in the lead and Richa thought he was heading for the market place. Instead, at the fork of the trail that would take them down to the market place, Kaluba stopped. They could see the laboratories in the distance. Kaluba spoke of the compound and what he had personally seen there at another time.

He described in detail, a man with the legs of a lion attached where the man's own legs should have been. Richa had never seen these misfits but had heard many stories about them. They could see movement across the compound that appeared to be human like, but could not distinguish the details. Kaluba told them he could tell by the stature that what they were viewing one of the misfits that survived the operation.

# EVIL VERSUS GOOD

Richa could not see clearly from this distance but could imagine the horror of such human destruction. The facial features of those that had been used in the experiments were said to be as gruesome as the animal parts that were attached. Often the features could not be distinguished as human from the contortions the facial muscles had gone through in pain. They watched the movement as the form lumbered across the compound and entered the laboratory out of view.

Richa prayed that God would allow them the right words to help the villagers refuse to succumb to the evil that was destroying Atlantis. Kaluba motioned for the group to follow and turned to walk up the trail that led to the top of the mountain and the priest's compound.

The group arrived at the priest's compound early in the day. Richa was thankful for the solace of her hut. It was calming to have the comfort of safety. As she settled in with prayer she reflected on the good and gave thanks for the time that she had to work with clays. She knew that God gave her visions to guide her with producing new creations to share with the others.

In the days and weeks ahead Richa continued to travel with Mikus and Federico to visit the villagers and on occasion to seek out the beaches. Sometimes Kaluba accompanied them. Richa loved her work with the villagers but also enjoyed going along the bay and combing the beaches for what lay in colorful arrays. She found pebbles that glistened and discovered that some were shiny in the day and also lit the night on their own. It was like God had shone his light of the day through the pebbles that continued to glow at night. These bright stones were calming to the mind.

Richa found that the light from the pebbles would also help those find the light of night. The light was dim but it was enough light to make a difference. She gathered all the pebbles she could find to make her creations from the visions that she saw. She understood that it was God's gift of showing her how to place these pebbles together in the formation of a flower in soft clay.

Back at the compound she put her ring of pebbles that she had encircled with clay into the fire. When the clay was fired to stone, the shiny pebbles were easily seen as a design against the hardened clay.

When she hung her designs of clay up for display, the pebbles could be seen shining at night and all day. She also used the dyes from flowers to color the portions of the clay that did not cover the pebbles. It was a unique process that allowed her mind to delve deep into her thoughts. She knew that she could look at the pebbles and use them to focus her thoughts.

She found that this deep focus with her thoughts allowed her to predict to others the future of their times. Her predictions of the future helped them find their own courses. Her own goals were set on helping others rid themselves of thoughts that would lead them to the evil on Atlantis, to control others. She gave the creations for them to meditate and find the peace of the soul. She helped many to mend their own beliefs before they were wasted in the ruin of the times from the evil.

Time passed quickly. Richa loved Atlantis' beauty and charm. She loved the freedom she had to explore the beaches. She especially liked the sea breezes that brought in the mists. The priests treated her with kindness and she learned so much from Kaluba. She liked her life that was attuned to helping others on this island.

Her great sadness was that they could not turn the evil away from the villagers. Each day there were stories of atrocities performed by the evil doers. Villagers would disappear into the night. Feasts and orgies continued in the villages where the evil ones could take control.

Their deeds were horrible. They spilled the blood of a lion into the midst of the blood of a man. They used the laboratories to search out ways to alter the blood of man. If the blood was mixed with that of a lion they thought that man would be linked with their eyes and have the sight of the animal. It was like creating a monster for their own selfish use.

The tiger's eyes, lion's blood and the cells of an elephant were all combined to grow strength. It all created a human that only an embryo would know. It was not an animal and it was not a human in its own respect but a blob that existed in a way that did not know its own human origins.

It was not a pretty sight to see the species altered. The evil scientists lost many humans and animals in their experiments. The water below the laboratories ran red many times from the carcasses and parts of both human s and animals that were thrown from the laboratories into the water below. No one knows how many were destroyed in such a way. The villagers only knew that the evil took man and woman alike for their own experiments and pleasure.

The priests knew that God would destroy the evil actions on those cliffs one day. They knew that all of Atlantis would be destroyed but they also knew that they would be led to safe ground. Knowing that it was only a matter of time before they would be led away, they focused their minds to helping villagers turn away from the evil.

The priests lived a simple life and were dedicated to God's ways. Their visions told them long ago that there would be a massive earthquake that would destroy all that remained on Atlantis. They understood the tremors from the earth that occurred frequently and were not frightened. They also knew that it would not be long before the shores of Atlantis would be washed away.

Richa too knew from God's messages, that he would destroy such a setting, because of the destruction it caused to so many. She was not afraid for her own safety but knew the time was growing closer to leave. When the day came that she would be told by God that the final days were here, she would gather her own strength to find her friends and move out of destruction's way.

Several years had passed by now. Richa never tired of Atlantis' beauty and charm. There were happy times along with the sadness of having the evil that lingered here.

As new people arrived on Atlantis looking for a good life she saw new villages spring up. There was plenty of food for all. The fruits were available and the villagers had an abundance of grains. There was always fish that could be caught and roasted over the fires.

The clays from the beaches made wonderful huts that the villagers shaped and linked together to formulate rooms. The huts were like little caves that represented the growth of the island. The villagers were artists in their own ways.

Besides the huts they made clay pots. They set up one area in their compound that the fires would not blow in the direction of the village, but traveled in another direction. It was a massive operation of many working the fires and the clay. They were artisans and carpenters at the same time.

Their villages were modern for those times. Even the cooking was set up in a way to allow many to use the fires. All had their own jobs to gather the fruits or the grains and fish that were plentiful. The food would be placed in shielded areas for each family to partake. They would choose their own food for the day and then cook it themselves and take it to their own huts for those waiting to be fed.

Richa noted that the women were treated as equals. They did not distinguish themselves as being lower than man but did adjust to the gathering of the food supplies. The men were the hunters that would find the catch of the day and then gather to tell their stories. The women ground the grains they raised and cooked the food. It was a happy lot except for the deception and the decay of the evil scientists. It could have been its own Eden, if they were allowed the tranquility of finding their own way.

Richa loved the priests and knew they were working for God in their own way. They lived a simple life and worked to find a way that might remedy the corruption that they were seeing. They helped many villagers see that the evil on Atlantis was not the calm that could take them down the right path to find the ways of God. They tried to help them choose their own desires in another way and to find that peaceful time. They encouraged them to find their own souls that God had meant them to see. Many of those souls eventually spread out into a new way and were saved from the destruction and were able to follow God's plan. In spite of their work, there were many others that looked away from the priests and chose to follow the path of the evil.

They were working for the good of man but it was impossible to penetrate the corruption on the inner island. On occasion Richa and the priests could see and hear the wild parties from their mountain perch but could not find a way to penetrate the minds of those on the inner island. These evil men were not willing to follow God's ways. This was an evil group who ran free and chose to take a stand against God and live on their own. It was a choice that was met with much disapproval. God's wrath was eminent and judgment would come.

It was not often that Richa made her way back down to the market place. When she did, Mikus and Federico always went with her. On one of their trips to the market they were surprised to see Captano, Leonardo, Baylona and the crew. They had much to share and spent hours telling each other of their experiences.

Because of Captano's new trade route his trips took him back regularly to their homeland in Italy. There was news of their families that brought special happiness to Richa, Mikus and Federico.

Richa learned her parents were both well and the family enjoyed prosperity with their farming. There was also sadness at learning that some of her family members had passed on since she had left.

It was tempting for Richa to return home with Captano but she felt in her soul that she could not leave until she was released by God's vision for her. She believed her release would only happen, when the last warning came before the fall that Atlantis was crumbling

# EVIL VERSUS GOOD

into the ocean. Leonardo understood but Captano only shook his head. He asked her how they would know to be there for her at the right time. Richa answered him by explaining that it was her faith in God that would bring it all together.

Mikus and Federico told Captano that they would be leaving when the priests left Atlantis. They considered themselves a part of the priest's family and would follow the group wherever it took them. Captano knew that there would be no changing their minds.

It was Leonardo that changed the subject and asked them about the villagers and the evil among them. It was a good feeling to tell someone from the outside of Atlantis and the cruelty here. If the word spread it might save someone that was tempted to follow the evil that existed. The five friends stayed up through the night discussing what Atlantis was like.

It wasn't until early morning when the skies began to light up that their conversation turned to food. Baylona was anxious to share with them some of his newest creations and set about stoking up the fire to cook what he had earlier found in the market place.

Such a feast they all had, but too soon it had to end and they said goodbye to their dear friends. Richa was exhausted but Mikus and Federico insisted that they travel back up the mountain trail to the village that they had visited when they first arrived on Atlantis. Baylona had given each of them a goatskin bag full of food for their journey up the mountain. The three became more aware of the need for water. Besides the food each carried a full goatskin bag of water.

It was afternoon when they walked into the compound of the village. There was the usual warm greeting from the villagers when they arrived. All three were exhausted and were happy when the evening meal was over and they could retreat to the huts that had been assigned to them.

After a refreshing sleep Richa, Mikus and Federico joined the villagers for an early morning meditation and prayers. Mikus led the group in the same chanting voice that Kaluba always did. Breakfast was a pancake from a grain that had been ground and cooked over a fire. The fruits were plentiful to go with the grain paddies.

After their meal Richa, Mikus and Federico remained in the village for the morning. The villager's had lost another loved one to the evil ones and were in despair from their loss.

The three had heard similar stories of loss so often. One of the villagers had been herding the goats in the fields near the village when a man with evil intent approached him. The man sat for a long time with the villager but when the villager stood up to leave he was grasped by the arm and pulled into the foliage out of view. Other villagers heard the ruckus and ran to help him but it was too late. They were gone and had taken the villager with them. His family knew that he would never been seen again.

Richa, Mikus and Federico spent time in prayer with the villagers. This same story was repeating itself over and over and it seemed that the villagers were never prepared or able to protect themselves against the evil. Richa began to question her own wisdom for not taking up arms to help the villagers in a more meaningful way to strike back.

She knew that God would answer all of her prayers in his own way.   On her return to her home on the mountain, Richa was determined that she would pray to God and ask why he allowed this to happen over and over again.

As the three approached the priest's compound the monkeys flew out from everywhere to greet them.  They saw Kaluba walking toward them among the monkeys.  All were happy he was there to greet them.

It was as if Kaluba had known of Richa's questions and was anxious to begin an afternoon session of learning.  She would later refer to this as receiving enlightenment from Kaluba."

ATLANTIS *A New View*

## CHAPTER IX:

### THE POWER TO DESTROY

"Kaluba, Richa, Mikus and Federico were surrounded by monkeys in the compound. It was Kaluba who was responsible for such frenzy. It was the smell of bananas that he was carrying in a basket of jungle leaves that had stirred up the monkeys.

There was a mischievous smile on Kaluba's face as he motioned for the three to follow him. The monkeys were like pied pipers and followed Kaluba in their exuberance to have their favorite fruit. Kaluba stopped off at the feeding area for the monkeys while Richa and the others watched.

The noise of the monkeys had disturbed the whole compound and the other priests appeared at doorways to watch the entertainment. One by one Kaluba peeled a banana and broke off a piece for a screaming monkey. The monkeys were scrambling to be first and it was true merriment for Kaluba, as he danced in circles to keep the monkeys from toppling him down.

All too quickly the bananas were gone and the monkeys disappeared into the trees. Kaluba raised his hands in delight and walked off in the direction of his own hut. Richa, Mikus and Federico all followed closely as they knew that a serious lesson was coming.

The three understood that somehow he knew Richa was looking for confirmation of why God allowed all the evil on Atlantis to continue. Richa thought Kaluba would begin the lesson with answers to her questions but he did not.

This is Kaluba's story that he begins with the earthquakes on Atlantis and why they continued to disrupt the quiet of the island."

He spoke. "Long before my time on this island the rumblings began on occasion. It was God's first warnings that he was displeased with the evil that man had brought down on mankind. The believers in God trembled but the evil men gave no heed. The evil ones believed they would control mankind with the power they held in the science of their hands.

The believers knew from the tremors that circulated the island that God had spoken to them as warnings to follow his ways. Yet many were not strong enough to protect themselves against the evil men and so mutilation of man continued.

There were other priests living on Atlantis other than the group you know now. They were the first priests to arrive on Atlantis with the hope of removing the evil from power with the power of words.

Remember the meaning of my words when I say to you that power comes in many ways. God, in his love for mankind, would never remove mankind's freewill but he did indirectly send special people who believed in following his ways. He knew that their gifts could be used to save others from following evil ways. One of these special people was John of the Nile. He represented God's own answers for others to use their freewill for developing their mind and knew that it was best for them to forgo the processes of evil to find a more enlightened way of life.

John came from the area of the Nile of Egypt. That is how he got his name, John of the Nile. He surfaced in his own homeland as the son of a king. His father's kingdom pronounced him, in the future, to have a crown.

# THE POWER TO DESTROY

*John was not always gentle in how he treated others. He used his power as a dictatorship and pushed the people into developing in ways that pleased only him as the king's son.*

*John was aware that his way of commanding action only brought enemies and grief to his kingdom. The change in his thinking came about when a group of priests visited his kingdom. They offered to aid John in finding a better way to manage a kingdom. Their influence was the turning point in John's life. They taught him that it was not the crown, that he possessed, which kept him free, but his own mind that could dictate to others the ways to find their own peace.*

*John listened to the priests and set about finding those that were open to his new thinking. He used this audience to deliver his speeches. In those speeches he developed a passion for clearing the minds of those that could not see God's ways. He spoke in a way to influence them but allowed them to use their own freewill to find their own good judgments.*

*John's commitment to others cleansed his own passions and renovated others into following his ways without a dictatorship. He allowed them to follow along with their own plans so they too could find a better path that would lead them to find their peace within and give them a clearer mind.*

*The Nile was John's home but he did not exist there for long. He found his power of speech was actually from the peace he held within. He had discovered that his own fortunes could come from his own mind in the attempts to free other minds. He knew that when he spoke, others could become mesmerized in desiring to follow his own passions towards God.*

*He believed that he had been sent priests to help him find the words for a kinder place for all. In his own awareness he found that others needed those words for a kinder place to grow. He said that God had sent him messages that he could use as his gift of speech to help others find new ways. In helping others it would also keep his focus on finding new audiences. It was in this mode that he felt pulled to distant Atlantis where the villagers needed his guidance.*

*John had become kinder in his thinking and was ready to spread his words to others to know God. He discovered that his delivered speeches were uplifting. He was an orator of sorts that took with him the wisdom that he knew had been held out to him by God. He knew that the words would only be justified if he used them for the good of preparing others.*

*He became a priest with a passion. His priesthood was a chosen faction by his own mind. He did not learn of those teachings from others but learned of those teachings from meditation that the priests taught him to use. It was in his own great spiritual growth and chosen field of orating those words to others that he believed that he had found his own placement to deliver God's own chosen words.*

*There were other influences in John's life other than the priests that he had met. His time in Egypt was after Moses but he knew the stories of Moses and how he had found his own placement in the rocks of a land covered by sand. He was compelled to learn why the effects of one man, Moses, had such a hold on those that looked upon him as a man of such wisdom. John too wanted to develop such wisdom to portray to others that they too are chosen to follow God's ways.*

# THE POWER TO DESTROY

*He studied Moses' ways for a time and learned of him self and how he had found God. In his new found mission in life he was determined to seek out the villagers of Atlantis. It was with this in mind that he said goodbye to his father and his kingdom to sail to Atlantis.*

*When John arrived there were other priests on this mountain where we now live but none as clairvoyant as John. He knew that the messages that came from his mind would only develop a clearer picture. Other priests that lived here accepted his words because they too knew that he had been touched by the presence of God.*

*John only wanted to inspire others with those words that were developed from his own mind. In this way others could formulate in their own minds their own perspective.*

*Atlantis, as a whole, was beautiful at that time but what it lacked was the will power among many to overcome the influences of the evil men that surrounded them. They did not find the messages from their souls that would have helped them follow the path of good with their freewill. When God saw the plans of the evil ones and knew they were trying to control all of mankind, he decided to send others to help guide the villagers in the right direction. He also warned them of the tremors that started shattering the ground of all Atlantis.*

*John of the Nile felt strong as a priest and set out to make a difference among the villagers. He took a chance and paraded around as an orator. When he spoke, he would have many that would follow him. It was like a big event in every village. Many of the villagers felt that they would become blessed with their own messages in their own heads when they listened to John's words of God. They thought then that they too were part of a bigger plan that would allow them to see a bigger picture. It was in this* caring and sharing that the views of the evil became clearer and many were saved.

John convinced many of the decay and blessed them with the words that only God had delivered to his mind. As hard as he worked to help, his speeches were not enough to turn all the villagers around and change their thinking.

He spent more time with those that found his speeches hard to follow. He would meditate and relate to them his own course. If he found that there were some that were weary of hearing him, he would go to them and ask them to pray to vacate their own minds of the trials that they had found on Atlantis. He asked them to use their minds to look into a clean slate and find a new awareness. It was like opening a book and they were the characters in that book and he would tell them how the story would unfold if they would look to God as the only God of their times.

All of the villagers that had heard John's speeches loved him and his presence was calming. His ways though were not always effective in making the changes that he was seeking. The villagers needed the serenity of their own minds to allow them to find peace for themselves.

The king and the evil men did not look at John as a threat for their own ways and allowed him to stay. They knew if he could persuade some villagers into his way of thinking there would be new villagers to take their places that would want the strength and power that they had promised. The evil men were aware of the influx of men to Atlantis from far away that were looking for what they offered. The new arrivals only brought new blood to the island for them to use for their experiments.

The evil in power on Atlantis did not take the time to hear John's words. They did not worry of the changes he brought about because they believed they would be the *chosen rulers when they developed a man that could not be destroyed by any other kind.*

*John never lost faith that his way would bring relief to those on Atlantis and stayed for a long time. He lived with the priests at this compound and learned their ways. He knew from the messages that he received that Atlantis would be destroyed one day. He was told it would be after his time and there was no need to depart until more effort was made to save the people. He helped many choose another life style and developed a plan for many families to gather into a more peaceful life.*

*John was on Atlantis for many years. As he grew older he longed to return to the Nile from where he had come. He planned to use his findings in Atlantis to develop a new sequence for others to follow in his own kingdom. He always felt blessed with the knowledge that God had led him to a fountain. He would never have found it if those words that God had delivered to him many times had not been listened to.*

*He returned to the Nile in Egypt in time to say goodbye to a world that he knew and to find another path to deliver peace to others. In time he passed on from old age.*

*I tell you this story of John because I want you to know that God never stops giving his messengers ways to help others. If they are not successful, it is because the recipients own freewill has gotten in the way.*

*I have a special message for you, Richa, in explaining to you why God, with his all mighty power, did not stop the evil on this island of Atlantis. You Richa and both you, Mikus and Federico must remember this message in all its content. You can draw on it in helping others with the same questions you have raised.*

*I feel that you already know and understand what I am about to tell you but that it will be a confirmation. This will be good for your mind to think of when you are giving your own messages to others.*

*Wherever there is good there is always evil and where there is evil there is always good. Knowing that evil and good exist brings to mind the explanation of why God, with his all mighty power, did not stop the evil on Atlantis. It is not in the power but in the peace of man that any evil can be absolved. If mankind does not have the peace within they will never rid the evil that lurks all around.*

*It is in the choices that we find that allows the mind to become at peace. The peace comes from choosing the good over the evil.*

*Evil lurks at every bend but evil can not be controlled by a mind that is not at peace. It is in that peace that wisdom seeps through to find that the mind can then develop that wisdom to find good.*

*If God were to interfere with that process, then evil would not only lurk around each bend but would disguise its ways as God's plan. In that way one would never be allowed to find the peace needed to overcome evil. Within the structure of freewill, we can develop our own way to find that peace for ourselves and we can outwit evil.*

*God did not leave it to chance, if we listen. He has given us visions and messages in the way of gifts, to use to prevent evil from growing. Using these gifts for good is following God's path to overcome evil, but it remains our choice to follow or not to follow. We know the difference between good and evil. We can understand that we must have peace within to fight evil.*

# THE POWER TO DESTROY

*The evil, on Atlantis, is working in ways to control mankind. If an individual uses their own freewill to repel the evil, they can find peace that will find goodness in life.*

*It was in man's freewill, that evil could not be destroyed by any other kind, but evil lurked further into the development of power, and that could rule over all other kinds. It is in that process that evil possesses a passion to control.*

*Our freewill that God has given us is the tool we can use. It is in the freewill of man that our minds can paint a clearer picture. We can not undermine freewill because it is our gift from God that allows us freewill to think.*

*When we deliver our own messages of peace to develop a plan for the good of others, we have developed a motion of peace and love to flow freely. It is in that flow of peace that mankind works on the positive currents to expand the goodness or light or energy that is controlled by the good of mankind.*

*It is through our own choices that we can manifest such a passage to control our own motions of peace to develop other motions of peace. We are the key to finding these motions by what we do and say that expands our own world into the love that is needed to carry it further.*

*When we do not follow God, there are always repercussions in unforeseen ways. It destroys our growth. The world does not expand in the right sequence because many souls have lost control. It is in that growth that we are made up of many to find a way to survive. It is like one of many controlling a time of growth.*

*It seems cruel that the evil men are mangling the bodies of the innocent with drugs and animal attachments and other experiments. It is cruel and God does know and sees it. He sees that man is destroying man and is angry.*

*He has sent good to overcome evil but has not interfered with our freewill to make choices. The tremors in the ground are warnings of what is to happen to the evil. What you Richa, Mikus and Federico do to help others overcome evil is your choice in following God's ways. There are others fighting evil in the same way as you. You see it among the priests and many of the villagers.*

*During these days of evil many are losing their lives. I know that seeing villager's lives taken by evil saddens you. Those that have lost their lives to such evil experiments have been taken into God's arms to live on in eternity in a better time. Those that control such evil are given free berth to change and to find peace for their own growth. Few of the evil ones on Atlantis have mended their ways.*

*You must note that God has not interfered in a process that carries on in evil ways except indirectly through those that chose to follow his ways. Even the tremors in the ground are meant as indirect warnings. These warnings have not changed the evils' ways. The growth of the evil has not subsided and there is now a risk that they will continue to destroy mankind..*

*The possibility of all mankind being destroyed with evil totally in control has God ready to use his own power to remove evil from power. His messages tell us that he will not allow all of mankind to be destroyed. He is now in the process of warning the evil ones with the earth's tremors. If they do not heed to his ways he will destroy earth's own crusts to remove the evil from the land.*

*The time for you to leave Atlantis is near. You must remain alert to God's messages. He will guide you and help you with saving many more. This island will be destroyed and it is up to you to follow a path to safety for yourself and all of those that will listen."*

"Kaluba stopped talking and lowered his head in meditation. Mikus and Federico followed. Richa knew that this was her cue that the lesson of enlightenment was over and she should return to her own quarters.

As if it was confirmation of all that Kaluba had said, the ground began to tremble under Richa's feet, as she hurried back to her own hut."

ATLANTIS *A New View*

## CHAPTER X:

## THE EXODUS AND FALL

"Richa spent each day on Atlantis, doing what she could to encourage the villagers to leave but now there was urgency about what she said. God had spoken to her as he had to the priests and the other believers. They were told that the island of Atlantis would crumble from the tremors very soon. In the end there would be large explosions from the earth's center crust that would demolish the island. When these blasts take place, the island and anyone remaining on it, would completely disappear into the sea.

The villagers were told there was time to leave the island and escape without loosing their lives. They were told the tremors were warnings and now the time was close. They must make preparations to leave in the next few weeks.

One day I heard Richa's thoughts asking God, would the fall of Atlantis come regardless of the earthquakes?

I don't think she was surprised at the message she received. God told her that the fall would not have come so abruptly, with the melting of the earth into its own core, had the evil that existed there subsided. God told her the key to destruction of all that remained was evil itself. Had they not been determined to continue to control all of mankind, the crumbling of Atlantis would have happened at a slower pace.

The priests and other believers were getting similar messages that alerted them of the destruction that would take place. God told them that their minds had been entwined in a plan to save the villagers. What they tried to capture was good with the use of their freewill and they must not suffer amidst the rubble of evil.

God warned of a sickness that would gain control over all of those that could not see. It would be through that sickness that many would not be able to control their own time. They would not, in the end, find their own souls and would be taken in the final eruption of Atlantis to another judgment beyond.

It was when the tremors circulated the island, that they all knew God had spoken the truth. The priests still moved among the villagers, as did Richa, to convince them that the end was upon them and they must leave Atlantis. The villagers were told that it was time to go to a place of safety. The earth would leave them in disarray if they did not heed the messages that God had sent.

The believers, among the villagers, also knew that Atlantis would soon fall into the ocean, from messages they had received. These villagers worked with the priests to convince the others that leaving was the only way to be saved.

The villagers had grown fond of Richa and the priests. Most believed that they had spoken clearly in an effort to spare them. They followed the priests closely when the rumblings and tremors began to come almost every day. They realized that the priests relied heavily on the messages they received and would alert the villagers up to the last hours to leave. Many were saved because of these last messages.

The believers knew that the tremors were another way God chose to alert them. The trembling of the ground was their confirmation. There were now huge portions of the island slipping into the sea from the movement of the ground. Havoc was all around.

## THE EXODUS AND FALL

Finally, Richa was told by God that she must prepare to leave within a few days. She asked Mikus and Federico to go with her but they declined. Their plan was to leave with the other priests when it was their time to leave. They had been told that the time for them would be when the crust was at its worst and when the rains would pour down daily in torrents. The waters from the oceans would rise to the heights of the waterfalls and then they would know it was time to leave. The waters would cover the surface of the island after that and there would be no time left to leave.

It became a mass exodus as the villagers scrambled to secure boats. It was not difficult though to find boats along the shores to take them away. There were many surplus boats found about the island that the villagers had used for fishing. The harbor was still full of merchant ships coming and going except they were leaving with men, women and children from the villages instead of products for trading.

They had heard the story of the fall that was coming to Atlantis. The same story was repeated over and over. Villagers were leaving Atlantis by now in frenzy. They were all seeking new homes in a safe place. The priests turned their hands into helping men, women and children load into boats that would take them to safe ground.

The usual still waters in the harbors were getting rougher as the tremors came more frequently. Seeing this was as much an alarm as the voices that Richa and the priests had heard. The villagers realized that if the waters got too high and rough, they would not be able to maneuver their boats in the strong currents and away from the island into open sea.

By now fall was coming in and the rains began pouring down, just as the messages predicted. One crisp morning Richa abruptly packed some of her rings of clay with the pebbles that produced light into a goatskin bag. These rings of clay with the shining pebbles would light the way as she traveled across the ocean to find her home in Italy. She had little else that she planned to take.

The sadness for her was to give her last farewell to Kaluba, Mikus and Federico and the other priests. It was sad for the priests to say goodbye also. They had all grown fond of Richa and treasured her friendship.

The priests assured Richa that they would listen and watch for the final warnings to leave. They planned to now take turns meditating through out the night and day as well as watch for the rise of the water. They had alerted all that would listen and they were now helping those leave by finding boats. They were also prepared to leave quickly.

Richa's friends asked her where she would go and she told them she would pursue her same plan to help others in another place. She told them that her first journey would be back to her home in Italy to visit her family. She would decide where she should be after that.

The priests told her that they too would go to a place that needed their help. They would find a place where mankind would be open to listening to the ways of God. What they had learned on Atlantis would be a part of their new plan to help others.

Mikus and Federico accompanied Richa down the mountain to the market place where they assumed they would help her locate a boat that would take her home. As they approached the market place they saw Captano's boat in the harbor. Richa was not surprised to see

## THE EXODUS AND FALL

Capitano and with him Leonardo and Baylona, but Mikus and Federico were amazed at his timing. Richa only said that she knew that if God had sent her messages to leave that he would also provide a means to do so.

Richa was amazed at how the waters had risen to cover most of the market place. There were few venders and those that were there were helping others load the boats with villagers that were leaving. Because the water was so high Captano had moored the boat closer into shore. He motioned for Richa to board as quickly as possible so that they could leave.

As Richa said goodbye and boarded the boat, she hoped that her path would again pass that of Mikus, Federico, and the other priests. As they parted from the shores Richa waved to her friends. She had a sense of loss. She was sad to leave such a place and sadder for those that were left behind.

The oarsmen quickly pulled the boat into the channel taking them just outside the harbor where the market place stood facing the inner island. She saw the castle and laboratories looming in the distance along the shores. She had heard that parts of the shore were crumbling around the castle and the laboratories but was surprised to see how much of the cliff had tumbled into the water below. She saw workers near the edge of the cliff trying to shore up parts of the castle and the laboratories that had crumbled under the tremors.

Richa sensed that it was close to the time that the last eruption would take place and the island would be lost in the sea. The oarsmen maneuvered the boat into the large channel that would take them out to the open sea. The waters were treacherous and if it had not been for the skill of Captano and his crew they could have been lost against the rocks at the edge of the channel. The boat finally cleared the channel into open seas. The swells in the sea were heavy but the oarsmen had the boat under control.

Richa sent up prayers thanking God for their safety and that the others leaving Atlantis would also find their way through the heavy seas.

Looking back at the outer ring of the island she was amazed that the beach was gone and that the water covered the pool of water that was once holding the waters from the falls. She watched closely as the island of Atlantis became smaller and smaller and their boat slowly moved the other way. The sea was full of boats carrying occupants to safety. Some were having more difficulty in the heavy seas than others, but they all seemed to be moving slowly out to open sea.

There were huge swells of water all around. The boat was like a cork in a bottle of water. They prayed to God to overcome their fears. Richa's thoughts came through to me as I listened. She had given her clay rings with the stones of light to Captano to light the way but she felt it was God's hand that was pushing them to safety and keeping them in a direct course to find their beloved Italy.

The rains had subsided and after a few days on the open sea, they sighted land and Captano decided, because of the turbulent seas, they should take refuge. His calculations were right. They were approaching a large landmass on the boot of Italy. The crewmen never wavered in their strength to oar along the coast until they found a large cove to retreat from the heavy seas.

Captano determined that they could leave the boat and hoped that it might be saved from the tidal waves

# THE EXODUS AND FALL

that were yet to come. He knew that it was not safe for all aboard to stay there. They must move back onto the mainland to higher ground. He expected higher tidal waves than he had ever witnessed, from the eruptions of Atlantis that was upon them.

Everyone carried what they could of the food supplies, sails and other items that Captano had aboard, in case the boat was lost to the sea. They climbed a trail high above the sea and took refuge in a cave on the face of the cliffs overlooking the bay below.

The rains began to fall again in torrents. They were thankful they were safely out of the weather. They settled in to wait for the first huge swells they knew would roll in. The waves rolled in one after another. They hit the face of the cliff where they had taken refuge. As the tidal waves hit, the spray from the force fanned out over the face of the cliff covering the entrance to their cave. Visibility from their lofty perch was impossible. Richa prayed for their safety as they huddled together inside the cave. Captano, with all of his experiences on the seas was overwhelmed at the sight of the largest waves he had ever seen. The only fear he had, was if the rocks on the cliff would come loose from the force of the tidal waves and hit them as they tumbled down.

They all felt that they were receiving the repercussions of the eruptions on Atlantis. All were sure that Atlantis must be gone. Richa was saddened at the thought and prayed that the others that were fleeing, were safe.

Finally the waters subsided and they could see clearly at the waters edge below. From this vantage place on the cliff, they could not see the small inlet that Captano had his oarsmen pull the boat into. He had left the boat to ride in this small inlet at the depth of the cove but was not sure that the boat had been safe from harm.

The group waited for the rains to let up. Finally, Captano gave the sign it was safe to leave the cave. They made their way back down the trail to get close enough to check out the boat. The debris that they saw along the shores was proof enough to them that all of Atlantis was gone. It would be many more days before they would receive any word of what had really happened.

They found the boat had been battered against the shores but was still afloat in the inlet. Captano had been clever in placing the boat deep into the inlet in the cove where the tidal waves were high but not as destructive. His boat had been damaged, but it was repairable.

In the days ahead, under Captano's deft directions, repairs were completed and the group could continue on their way. The experience they had all encountered would remain in their memories. Captano would add this story to his other sea stories as he proudly proclaimed the strength of his boat.

They continued to slowly oar along the shores of Italy toward home port on the west shores of Italy. They could easily see that the tidal waves had hit the coast in a rampage. Captano was not surprised at the damage that was done. There were many changes in how the land looked from the loss of soil and rocks that the high tidal waves had taken out to sea. Many villages along the edge of the water were all but destroyed. Those damaged the most were the ones that bordered the edge of the shores.

Captano made many stops along the shores at the ports where there once stood thriving fishing and trading villages. They found that many lives had been lost because the villagers did not realize that the tidal waves were coming.

Many fishermen and merchants had lost their boats to the sea but some boats were protected in inlets. They were damaged but could be salvaged. They were grateful that Captano was willing to help them. With him and his crew, many repairs could be made.

While the work was underway Richa used the time to console those that had lost loved ones and helped them pick up their lives in a positive way. She had a calm about her that gave them an inner strength.

As they finished work at one port, Captano moved to another port to help the villagers in anyway that he could. Months went by before Captano and his crew could break away from the many stops and take a direct route to homeport. At each village they heard stories about Atlantis. Merchants brought news of others as they journeyed by boat on their trade routes.

Atlantis was the talk of everyone. Captano and his crew alike were like the newspapers of today. There were stories about those that had left before the last eruption of Atlantis. There were those who said that they had seen the empty sea where Atlantis had once stood.

It was a marvel that there were stories of the priests and how they were one of the last boats leaving before the last eruption. Richa was delighted to hear that Kaluba, Mikus, Federico and all the priests were safe on the island of Crete. They had all left Atlantis just a couple of days after her departure. It was said that the sea had swells as big as mountains making it almost impossible to maneuver the boats. Richa smiled when she was told that each boat carried a ring of lighted pebbles of fire that helped light the way on a direct track to Crete.

There were stories of the last days on Atlantis and how the king and the evil men had made no move to leave. They continued to scoff at God's warnings. Witnessing the further crumbling of the castle and the laboratories from small eruptions did not undermine what they believed was their own power to control.

The priests had told others that the king and the evil ones were still there when they left and the priests believed they had been the last boats to leave before Atlantis erupted. It was God's words that echoed through the destruction, that they would be destroyed if they did not change their ways. It was their own convictions that held them down to be lost in the sea.

The stories Richa and the others heard were acts of heroism and bravery by the villagers to save their own. Sadly there were also stories of villagers that had refused to leave. There were leaders in the villages that believed the evil and thought their power was greater than any other. It was their free will that kept them on Atlantis. In the end, it also took the lives of innocent men, women and children that believed in what the King had said.

The birds took flight from the island. Richa had seen the skies filled with many birds as she left Atlantis. They had their own instinct that saved them.

The animals were not so fortunate. They had instincts to leave and many had swum out to sea early when the tremors came. Others hid in the jungle and it is believed that they all perished.

Richa then knew from the stories of others that Atlantis was gone forever. She knew that God had alerted many to flee. She was saddened for those that did not leave and was saddened by those that were destroyed by Atlantis and all of the evil.

## THE EXODUS AND FALL

The work at the last port on the south of Italy was completed and Captano took a direct route for the channel that would take them to the west coast of Italy. The oarsmen pulled the boat through and they all knew that homeport was close at hand. They were thankful for a safe journey and were happy to be landing in homeport. Captano and his crew made it home, but the journeys for Richa, Leonardo and Baylona were still ahead. They were anxious to see their families and set out on foot as soon as they could.

It seemed to Richa that it had been a long time that she had traversed this same trail with her friends in such high hopes of seeing Atlantis. In reality it had been almost eight years since she left home. She had seen much and learned more than she could imagine from her experiences and from the priests on the mountain. She especially had fond memories of Kaluba and his stories that always included a new awareness of God's ways.

On their journey back home, Richa talked little of Atlantis because it made her even sadder at the loss of lives and the destruction of the island. She was eager to see her family and begin life again to help others.

When the three approached the village, all of the villagers gathered around them to greet them and to hear all of their stories of Atlantis. She found that her siblings had grown and left to start their own families. Her parents had grown weary from age but they were well.

Leonardo and Baylona went on to spend some time with their families but it was understood that soon they would leave. They would travel back to the west coast of Italy and meet up with Captano. Together they had plans for a new trade route and were eager to work it out with Captano. It was easier for Richa to say goodbye as she knew she would see them again when they returned to see their own families as often as they could.

In the months ahead Richa found that her family had acquired even more land than they had when she left. The lands that were acquired were vast and stretched out into the interior. She took solace in knowing that it had produced plenty for her family. There was great pride in knowing that her family readily shared what they harvested with others.

As time went on it was easier to talk about Atlantis. She was saddened by the lives that were lost but tried to dwell on the good that she had found. She used the lessons she had learned from living on Atlantis to be useful in bringing a new awareness to others.

Richa took up life much as she had before she went to Atlantis. She meditated often and shared her visions with others. Her days were spent making clay objects for others and sharing her stories. Her family still thought of her as a priestess. She told them she was only a messenger of God's ways but they were not convinced. She left them with that belief. She determined the importance was in what she did and not in what she was called.

Richa knew it was right for her to be at home and was satisfied with her life for a time. Her contentment could not last long as her wandering soul needed a new place to grow. She had heard that Egypt was a place where many gathered from many places and were open to new ways. She determined this was a place that she could share her awareness in finding new ways to grow. She was intrigued by the possibilities of using her own art form for others to use as symbols to become aware of God.

## THE EXODUS AND FALL

Her final decision to leave her homeland came to light when Leonardo and Baylona returned home from one of their trading voyages with Captano. In her mind the timing of their visit was a message from God, that it was time for her to reach out to others in far away Egypt.

Her friends told her that Captano had established a new trade route that took them to Crete and then to Egypt. There was another journey planned to go to Egypt with Captano when they returned. Captano had sent word that Richa was welcome to go with them. He said that he would make a special side trip for her to view the area where Atlantis had once stood.

Richa felt that God had given her a gift to travel and she must not give that gift back. This journey to Egypt was one that she must take. She had saved a few of the bright pebbles of light from Atlantis and set about making rings of clay and inserting the pebbles for light to use on the journey ahead with Captano.

Richa knew that she was approaching the middle of her own life span and she must go while she had the energy to continue her work. She also knew her parents were aging and she would never see them again. She prayed for the right answer and found it would be her own freewill that had the final decision. She realized that she could not let go of what she called her own calling.

Saying goodbye this time was much more difficult than it had been before. She loved her family and knew they supported her calling. She promised to send messages back with Leonardo and Baylona. Her family was saddened to see her leave but put up a brave front as they waved goodbye to her. They were proud of her and she always remained in their minds as their own priestess."

ATLANTIS *A New View*

Captano told Richa that if his calculations were right, they should be over Atlantis. Though it was no longer there, you could almost see it.

ATLANTIS *A New View*

# CHAPTER XI:

## LIVES AFFECTED BY ATLANTIS

"Richa, Leonardo and Baylona set out on the same trail that they had crossed before walking to the west coast. It was Richa's third time, but for the other two it was one of many times that they had returned from voyages at sea to their home.

The three friends traveling by day found the trail to be dusty in the beginning. As they progressed along the trail and turned to the west, the trail wound through hills. The trail took them to a higher level and into stormy skies. They hoped for a rain so that they could replenish their drinking water between the villages along the way. Baylona was alert of the basins of rocks along the trail that held springs, but those were few and far between. He too hoped for squalls of rain so that they could replenish their fresh water.

Rain did come in downpours and they were able to catch fresh water. The rain did not last long but long enough to catch the water and to become drenched. As the sun peeked out of the clouds above them, they were warmed. They found that the trails held a damp freshness that cut the dust underfoot.

In the evenings Baylona did what he was good at and that was to cook. He always provided them with fresh meat. Sometimes that was rabbits and sometimes other unusual meats but to Richa and Leonardo it was always tasty.

Richa kept them amused with her many stories. She used pebbles that she carried to make a temporary chart to forecast their arrival in Egypt. Leonardo and Baylona were intrigued by her knowledge.

They were welcomed warmly at the villages where they stopped. The villagers were anxious to spend as much time as they could with them. They seemed to know that all three had visited the now famed fallen Atlantis. Richa was respondent to the many questions about Atlantis that she was glad to talk about.

She was only uncomfortable when the loss of villagers and children came up. She longed to hear Kaluba's voice and his wise display of words. Richa's heart, after all of this time, still ached for the loss of the innocent.

She understood that the evil whose plan it was to control mankind was the reason God allowed Atlantis to be destroyed. She felt a heavy weight of guilt for not doing more to save the innocent. Many times she had prayed to God for answers and always received the same vision. She saw a figure in a robe telling her to have patience and she would find her answer in time. Deep in her mind she was in hopes that the time to understand would come when Captano took her by boat to view the site where Atlantis once stood.

The companionship of the three friends and their stops at the villages along the way made time on a long trek pass by quickly. Captano was waiting for them and was happy to see that Richa had joined Leonardo and Baylona. He too was anxious to travel to Egypt but was looking forward for other stops including the one at the fallen Atlantis.

With final farewells, Captano instructed his crew to head out to sea. It would be a long journey from what we know today, but Captano looked at it as a short journey. At that time of year much of the journey by boat would be from the sails moving them along at a faster clip than the oarsmen could have. He smiled proudly when he thought of his beloved boat and bragged openly that it was hand hewn. Such a boat, he acknowledged, was strong against any sea. His courage was evident but it was also evident that he looked realistically at the wrath of a storm driven sea. He was always attentive to the change in the weather. At night he used the stars and Richa's clay circle of shining pebbles to guide them.

Richa respected Captano and trusted his decisions but she also sent up prayers that God would give them a safe journey. She felt it was God's strength that would protect them against the sea. It was in her belief that he was with them the entire way.

Captano made land stops at small islands in the sea to trade and to give his crew a deserved rest. Richa believed these stops were a part of God's intended plan so that they could all have time to share along the way.

Captano was familiar with the islands where they stopped. He marveled at the changes since Atlantis fell and explained how much bigger the land mass had been before the eruption. The villagers had their own stories of their loss and how they managed to survive on an island that was nearly covered with tidal waves. Richa was especially interested in how they had gathered together, what was left, and how they had rebuilt their lives. She would remember their many struggles and would use what she learned to repeat to others the positive attitudes of these hardy villagers.

As they left their last island stop, Captano headed the boat to a more southeasterly course. The seas had become very calm and the sky overhead was clear of clouds. It was almost an omen to the silence that awaited them.

It was a beautiful day and the sun was sparkling on the water. The wind had died down. Captano spoke to the crew to bring down the sails and motioned for the oarsmen to take the oars. They automatically took up the rhythm. It was silence all around, except for the sound of the oars dipping and being pulled through the water. In a short time Captano raised his hands for the men to stop oaring. He turned to Richa and told her if his calculations were right, they were now over what was once the center of Atlantis.

The memories were too much for Richa and she was overcome with grief. With tears streaming down her face she prayed to God for the souls that were lost when Atlantis fell.

Captano, Leonardo and Baylona moved away from her as far as they could to give her a moment. Except for Richa's emotional prayers the silence was erie. Looking down into the depths of the water Richa felt so small and so insignificant. She prayed again as she so often had in the last years for better answers to why the innocent villagers and the children were lost. In answer to her prayers, she saw a reflection in the water. It was the same vision she had seen before of a man in a robe and she heard the same voice telling her she would have her answer in time.

She looked toward Captano, Leonardo and Baylona thinking they might have seen the same vision. They were quietly talking about Atlantis and by their voices she knew they had not seen the vision she had.

She moved closer to the three men. She felt she needed to join them and to hear their voices to break her grief and the absolute silence all around. As she moved across the boat she felt a presence that was calming. The presence gave her relief from the grief she felt.

Captano and the others all began to speak to her at the same time. It was as if they too felt the same presence that Richa felt, as they spoke of the power of what had happened there. All in their own way, they shared how the impact on their minds, came from having survived a catastrophe of such a magnitude, as the fall of Atlantis.

Richa's experience on Atlantis confirmed her belief that her purpose and calling was to help others find their own awareness. She was confident she was doing the right thing in going to Egypt. It was her desire to find another place where she could help others. Returning to the site of Atlantis brought back horrifying memories of the loss of lives but with the feeling of a greater presence, she now felt calm. It helped her to remember that there had also been good among the evil. In many ways the good had overcome evil. She believed her experiences on Atlantis were meant to be and yet she was haunted with the thoughts that she should have done more.

The crew joined with the others and they talked of their lives since the fall of Atlantis and how each day was more precious. How their families were the most important things in their lives. How they felt drawn to an awareness of knowing the evil among the good. They felt the need to live their own lives in a way that would protect others from the evil on Atlantis from ever happening anywhere else.

In the quiet, after hours of discussions, it was Captano that motioned for the oarsmen to take up the oars. This had been a good thing, stopping here in a sea of silence with all the memories. To Richa, being here and sharing with the others had raised her spirits and she was now certain that she was following the right path in going to Egypt to help others. The vision that she saw and had seen so many times confirmed again that she would have better answers in God's own timing.

Captano took a due southerly direction. He told them that the next stop would be the Island of Crete. The wind had not picked up and the oarsmen were at the oars constantly to keep the boat moving. Richa was tired of watching the waves splash against the boat and she drifted off to sleep, dreaming of a new life in Egypt. It was dawn when Captano gave the oarsmen a rest. The sea was still quiet and the boat rocked gently in the calm of the waves while the men got a deserved rest. Moving by oar alone was slow and it would be several days before they would arrive at their next stop.

Finally the Island of Crete was spotted in the distance. The sun was out and the sky was blue. Captano spoke of the island as being tropical, much like Atlantis. In spite of the tide the oarsmen easily pulled the boat into a small harbor. They could see that they were approaching a market place on the shores. They were greeted warmly by the merchants and villagers. The merchants knew that Captano had brought trade goods that were popular among them and the villagers.

Their arrival like at most ports would be celebrated with a feast. Some of the villagers quickly dispersed to set it up while others clamored for a look at the trading goods that Captano had aboard. They spotted Richa and were surprised to see a woman in the robe of a priest.

The bold ones were anxious to talk to her and crowded in for a closer look. Richa understood their quizzical looks and told them with a smile that she had come from her homeland in Italy. She then broke the ice with her stories and they were intrigued. From that moment on she was given the title, Priestess, as she not only looked like a priest but she also spoke like one.

Soon the feast was set out on long tables. Baylona had been in his glory, helping in the preparations. He had an opportunity to share his knowledge of the art of cooking. In a short time the call came for them to eat.

As Captano and his group made their way to the tables set out for the evening feast it was Richa that gave out a surprised cry. Coming into the compound was Kaluba, Mikus and Federico followed by the other priests. Richa was overwhelmed with joy. She knew that the priests had found their way to Crete after the fall of Atlantis but did not know that they were still there. She had heard they had planned to go to the mainland of what is now Turkey and felt they had already left.

They greeted each other like family. They were all overjoyed to see each other. The villagers on Crete were wonderful and warm but it was Richa's old friends that she embraced the most. They had all shared so much on Atlantis and they had been a part of her life everyday.

There was so much to talk about. It would have been easy to forget the feast the villagers had laid out if they had not urged Richa and the priests to move up to the tables of food.

In the excitement they had become oblivious to their role as guests. It was not their intent to be rude. Richa and the others were grateful for the kind reception that was offered them. She could see the table of bountiful fruits that had been laid out. The bananas reminded her of Atlantis. They were her favorite fruit and she had not had them since Atlantis. Kaluba told her these fruits were grown on Crete. Now she understood Captano when he had said that the climate on Crete was like the climate on Atlantis.

After they had all eaten their fill the villagers invited them to join them to tell their stories. Story telling was a common practice after a feast and the villagers followed the same format as other villagers had on their route. There was a huge fire in the middle of the compound and everyone gathered as closely around it as they could. The guests were asked to share their stories of their journeys and of Atlantis.

Captano, then Baylona and Leonardo obliged by talking about what they knew best. Captano spoke of the strength of his boat and the strong arms of his oarsmen under wild seas. Leonardo spoke of the courage of Captano and the devastation at the other islands along the way from the tidal waves. Baylona was impressed by the foods that had just been served and spoke of how this feast reminded him of the bountiful fruits and meats on Atlantis at the market place.

When it came Richa's turn, she spoke of the most spiritual part of their journey, which was the stop at the sight of Atlantis. She told them what it meant to her to return to the place where Atlantis once stood. She described the landmass that had once stood there and how the sea covered all traces.

She told them that being on the spot where the silence was now eerie had brought memories flashing back in her mind to the time she had spent on Atlantis. She explained the evil that had existed there and how they took over the lives of the villagers. Richa talked of how the priests had worked to bring an awareness to the villagers in how to escape the evil. They were told they could use their own freewill to save themselves from submitting their bodies to the evil to be used as experiments.

Richa spoke of the many tremors felt that were the warnings from God that the plans of the evil to take over mankind would never be allowed. Some listened and abided and some did not.

Near the end, the priests were told by God that the last eruptions were coming. They warned the villagers and many left but there were also many that stayed until the last eruption and it was too late to leave. Richa's emotions welled up and with tears she said how devastated she was at the loss of lives and how she felt she should have been able to do more to save more villagers, especially the children from being lost. She told them of her vision of the man in a robe. He had told her to be patient and she would have her answer in time.

The group was awe struck at her story. They could see in her face and voice that her grief was real. To regain her composure she asked Captano to speak. She would join Kaluba and the other priests. Their presence would lift her spirits.

She had seen Kaluba and the other priests among the group as she talked but now they had disappeared from her sight. She was afraid she would not see them again and moved off into the night in search of Kaluba and the other priests.

Leonardo caught up with her to tell her that Kaluba left word that he would meet with her in the morning. He had told Leonardo that while they were safe among the village members outside of the city palace, if they were seen to linger too long someone would surely notify the king. Here on Crete, the king within the city palace, was also considered a priest and led his people with only his own beliefs that were different than those of the priests.

Richa returned to the group by the fire. Captano was holding the group of enthusiastic listeners as he continued telling his favorite stories. It was very late into the night before the group finally broke up to return to their own homes. Richa had been invited to spend the night at the home of one of the villagers and she was grateful.

Very early the next morning Richa left her new friend's home to meditate in the compound near the warmth of a huge fire. As she meditated it was Kaluba that tapped her on the shoulder. Mikus and Federico were both with him. They joined Richa in meditation. Kaluba began chanting as Richa had heard him so often do on Atlantis. She noted that both Mikus and Federico meditated with the same kind of chanting as Kaluba.

Soon the villagers appeared and asked them to join them for the morning meal. They gratefully accepted. When they had finished, Kaluba indicated to Richa that he would like to speak to her away from the group. Together they moved to a quiet place. Kaluba began with what Richa recognized as a lesson from a wise one."

*" I have heard you speak of your visit to where Atlantis once stood and I would now like to recap the last moments as I left with the other priests. The day you left we were finalizing our last calls to the villagers and we were urging them to leave immediately for safety. Many more did leave but there were others that did not. We too prayed that we could save everyone but we also realized, as you must, that there was only one choice. The earth was moving with tremor after tremor and it was time to leave.*

# LIVES AFFECTED BY ATLANTIS

*The villagers were warned but it was their freewill that gave them the choice to stay or to leave. Just as it was your judgment to leave when you were told the time had come. Remember, while you were bringing awareness of God to many minds, you were also liberating their minds to know the right way to follow God's ways. It was in that liberation of their minds that they could have conquered an awareness to remain on earth.*

*These villagers took with them in the memories of their souls that they would live on in another time, and have the knowledge of what could have been. The lesson is there for them to draw on in another time that their own freewill destroyed their time on earth and not from the hand of anyone else.*

*As to the innocent children that were lost; you must not grieve. God has a special place for them. It was not their innocence that was lost, but it was a liberation that* **allowed their mind and soul to conquer another time and that became their justification. Those same children will again live in another time to find that what they learned from having been involved in the fall of Atlantis was liberation into another life. It gave them ways to seek out their own justice, not in losing an earthly life, but learning from the mistakes that were made and from knowing that knowledge will be kept in their own souls. That knowledge will keep them from the same fate that would not allow them to have their own rights by the destruction of someone else's freewill."**

**"Kaluba stopped talking and Richa knew the lesson was over. She thanked Kaluba for the enlightenment and realized this was the answer to her grief. She exclaimed to Kaluba that he was the man in the robe that she saw in her vision! He only smiled but she knew it was true.**

Richa saw Mikus and Federico coming toward them. In her happiness from the words that she had heard from Kaluba, she asked if he and the other priests would be willing to join her in Egypt.

Kaluba waited for Mikus and Federico to join them before he replied."

*"You know that we came here to Crete just before the fall of Atlantis. We had little time to warn the villagers that huge tidal waves were coming. It was a warning that saved many lives but there were many others that were lost.*

*All along the coast and even the palace city on the hill, there was danger of being destroyed by the fury of the sea. They knew well enough to get out of the way because they had felt the wrath of the sea before but there was little time for a total exodus.*

*We too had to flee to higher ground. We watched the pounding of the waves from a vantage point that was safe. It was too late to help more to higher ground.*

*In the days ahead we were looked at with kindness because of the warnings we brought but it did not last long. Our beliefs were different than the kings and he was considered the priest of the people he ruled.*

*We did not judge him and the villagers that had different beliefs. We judged them only for their needs. We were there to console the souls in such a time and we analyzed the surrounding damage. The king did not see it that way and we left for the hills to join other priests in seclusion.*

*We set up a new life for a time in a makeshift way to disguise ourselves from being found. There were villagers that approached our habitat and for the most part they were kind but not ready to hear about our ways.*

# LIVES AFFECTED BY ATLANTIS

*Over time we met with others outside our home. There were those that did not believe in us and there were those that saw our life as a new awareness. For the most part our time has been used for evaluating and teaching among ourselves those things that we learned from Atlantis.*

*Mikus and Federico are now priests, and will join us in our plans. Our beliefs here are different but we have decided to find a place with those that do not believe I the times set forth, but will listen to God's ways. We are needed in a place where souls will grow and our calling will help them survive.*

*We will find a path to circulate our knowledge and to share the messages that we have received. It is a new calling that we have all agreed on to find a new road. We know that God will reach out and guide our movements so that we can proceed in the right direction if we listen.*

*Our plan is to proceed across the sea to the east into a new climate in the mountains. There are villagers whose minds are open and awaiting our messages. We can help in that way. Our new journey will not take us in your direction but you shall be in our prayers and we will miss you.*

*Your own calling is genuine and your beliefs are sound. Your own strengths are in following God's ways and you will do much to help others. It is not in sadness that we must say goodbye but in rejoicing in that our callings are clear."*

"**Kaluba stood up to leave and Richa knew this was goodbye. Her life had been enriched by this friendship. She had a last gift to give each of them. She drew from the pocket of her robe one of her shining stones that was attached to a makeshift chain. She placed one around the neck of each of her friends. She told them that the** lighted stones were only a reminder of the light they carried in the messages they had to share from their souls.

    Richa watched as her friends disappeared up the trail. She knew this would be the last time she would see them but her memories of them would be forever.

    She returned to the shore where Captano and his crew were loading the boat. Captano looked her way and told her it would be early tomorrow that they would be leaving.

    Richa smiled and nodded her head. She was ready. Her spirit was soaring and she was ready for whatever she might find at the next stop that was to be her home."

# LIVES AFFECTED BY ATLANTIS

## ANCIENT EGYPT

A paradise of sand and soil that melted into
a tropical oasis for all.
A paradise of beauty for those souls,
together as one marking their own call.

ATLANTIS *A New View*

## CHAPTER XII:

## EGYPT AFTER ATLANTIS

"Captano was right when he had told Richa that they would be leaving Crete early in the morning for Egypt. The harbor was dark and the only light was from the sun coming up as the oarsmen pulled the boat away from shore heading for the open sea.

Actually Richa was glad they were leaving early and there was no one seeing them off. If the priests had come, it would have been difficult to say goodbye again. She would miss them but she knew that they had their own calling to find others that desired to hear their messages. It was sad to think that their paths may never cross again in this life but the lessons she had learned from them would remain strong in her mind. The times they shared on Atlantis bound them together and would remain in all their memories forever.

There was enough of a breeze in the air that Captano ordered the sails raised. It would be a short journey to Egypt. Richa would use this time to converse with both Leonardo and Baylona about the island of Crete. They all agreed that the people there were far advanced culturally, than most islands they had seen, except for Atlantis. It was mutually agreed that those that fled from Atlantis to Crete were responsible, in part, for the advancements in crafts and the arts that the people of Crete enjoyed.

The three friends talked of the city palaces and the different kings that were in control over the island. How, in such a land of strong dictatorship, it was very difficult for new ideas in religion to be introduced. How this was reason enough for the priests to move on to find a people more open to listening.

They talked of their future plans. Leonardo and Baylona intended to continue following the trading routes with Captano. The two friends spoke of a desire to journey by boat down the Red Sea and beyond to the land we now know as India.

Richa planned to take up life very much as she had in Atlantis. She would reach out to those that were seeking. She thought that her experiences would be useful in explaining the processes one goes through to find their own way.

Sharing made the sailing time to Egypt go quickly. Only a few days had gone by when Captano announced the sight of land and ordered the crew to take down sails. He indicated they would be landing at an island off what we now know as Alexandria. He explained that the harbor around the island and in the port of Alexandria was too treacherous for a boat of his size to enter. The waters were shallow with protruding rocks just below the surface and there were coral reefs that had to be crossed. The going would be slow from now on until they took anchor at a distance from the shore. There would be small Egyptian row boats that would transport everyone to shore.

As they got closer in, Richa could see that it was a place of great activity. Many boats were coming and going. Captano told her that this was a seaport of great importance where trade goods and people arrived and left on a daily basis. The boats carried the trade goods from India and China and other faraway places. He told her she would see silks that would be as amazing and bright in colors as she had seen on Atlantis. There would be other marvels to behold such as clothes woven from grasses and fine golden necklaces and bracelets crafted by the people that live there.

It was quite thrilling for Richa. As their boat was brought in closer and closer to land she could see the outline of the mainland in the distance. The green seemed to be laid out in a valley. It was as if the valley met the ocean and that the green met the blue without any hesitation. Captano told her that this was the valley of populous for Egypt where many people lived. He told her that the land outside of the valley was barren with sand stretching out into the distance.

Slowly the oarsmen edged the boat toward shore. She saw the many rocks just under the surface of the water and understood why Captano had said the port was treacherous. Captano watched every move and was happy when it was time to tell the crew to drop the anchor into the water.

Approaching them, were Egyptians in small rowing crafts. They were coming to take them ashore. Captano had stopped in a sea of other boats anchored in place. There was great activity all around and Captano told Richa this would be goodbye for now and that he must stay with the boat. Leonardo and Baylona would be going with her on the short trek to the mainland. Richa looked at him quizzically and he smiled. Before us you can see a wide land mass. This mass of land connects this island with the mainland. You have to follow the trail along the waters edge to reach the mainland.

Captano told Richa that he was concerned for her safety. He had landed here many times and knew of the forces that lived in makeshift shelters along the water. They were a rough lot and lived off others good luck.

ATLANTIS *A New View*

They stole anything they could find whenever they saw an opportunity. Captano wanted to see her safely with the others that believed as she did.

Richa understood his concerns and was comforted by this. It would be right to be with others that believed as she did. She expected also to find villagers she had known that had fled from Atlantis.

Leonardo and Baylona were instructed to follow the path to the mainland and continue around the bay to a colony that resided near the water. Captano, for the first time, embraced Richa in a fatherly hug to wish her well. As bold and courageous as he was, his heart had a soft spot for Richa and treated her like his daughter.

Richa assured Captano that she would find her way back to the port in search of his boat from time to time. Knowing they would see each other again, made it easier for the two friends to say goodbye to each other.

After the Egyptians took Richa, Leonardo and Baylona to shore in row boats, the three friends set out along the path toward the mainland. They passed by many people living in huts. They seemed to be wrapped up in their own way of life and did not greet the three. Perhaps it was Richa's long brown robe that made them wary, thinking that she was a priest. Whatever it was she was glad they were ignoring the three as they passed by.

The huts they saw were built in a makeshift manner from grasses, just as Captano had said. Richa was amazed that people were actually living in these grass shelters. They were flimsy and not put together well to resist the winds. She knew that the huts would protect the people from the mists but not the heavy rains and winds that came in off the ocean.

In spite of what she saw, Richa felt she had again found her oasis. Perhaps she could one day help these people to build better shelters with mud and sand. She was renewed in knowing she had God's work to do. As they reached the mainland the populace of people along the water grew in numbers. The huts in this area were sturdy and closer together. As they walked along the shore their path took them through a large village. The scene soon turned from huts that opened out into a market place at the harbor's edge. Small row boats were coming in and going out in the harbor. This market place seemed to be the hub of activity in Alexandria. They walked passed row after row of hawkers selling their wares.

Baylona's eyes lit up because of the variety of fruits and vegetables that were in the market place. Leonardo saw it as a place with a bountiful array of goods for trading. Richa saw it as a place to bring the wares she intended to make and to mix with the people.

The villagers were different than the people living along the landmass that connected the island to the mainland. The villagers all seemed busy and to have a purpose that centered on the same goal and that was to trade goods. They were friendly and spoke with all three.

As they talked, the same question always seemed to be asked as to where they had come from. When they found the three had come from Crete they were eager to hear news of the world outside of their harbor.

This village and market place already pleased Richa. This was Alexandria, a place she would learn to know well. She was interested in the villagers at the market and tarried to listen to their stories. It was Leonardo that urged Richa to continue along the waters edge away

ATLANTIS *A New View*

from the market to a calmer place. He promised her that it was not far to the colony. The two men were anxious to place her in the hands of the colony where they knew she would be safe. She could return to the market place anytime.

Leonardo was right, they had not walked far until they reached a quiet village that stretched out along the shore and stood almost independent of Alexandria. They were greeted warmly. It was as if they had been expecting them and had prepared a place for her to stay. She felt an immediate part of this colony and knew that these people would be accepting of her ways.

Leonardo and Baylona stayed for a few days until they were sure Richa was settled in. They took part in erecting a hut for her that she could call her own to live in.

All too soon for Richa the hut was completed and Leonardo and Baylona announced their departure. As the two friends left they promised to keep in touch with Richa as often as their trade route brought them back to Alexandria. Richa wished them happiness in their choice to travel with Captano as they all followed the trades. She would miss them but she knew she would see them again many times. She would look forward to sharing stories of her new life here in Alexandria.

It was easy for Richa to settle into life in this colony. There were many that quickly became her close friends. They enjoyed her stories and her visions. They looked at her as a priestess who willingly shared her experiences.

Richa visited the market place often and chuckled when the Egyptians also considered her as a priestess of sorts. She was not an appointment of the church but her reputation as a spiritual guide had followed her with the friends who fled Atlantis to live in Egypt.

She told them it was true that she had many visions from God to guide her every move. It was all right that they thought of her as having these messages by faith but they must know that the right to view them was her gift from God. She told them that the messages were meant to be uplifting and full of inspiration. In this way, she told them that many others would find their own gifts from God.

Richa fit into the same patterns that she had in Atlantis and that was to help others in anyway that she could. I heard her tell many in the colony that they must understand that Egypt was different than other lands. It was a land of many changes and many could not see through the darkness of the times. She warned them that they were only safe in this environment because of their belief that God would protect them. Those in control of Egypt looked at them as a small number and would leave them alone if their powers were not challenged in any way.

I watched and listened to Richa as she grew strong in her own way to reach out to others in this place that is called Alexandria today. It was a calm place to work and to rest and meditate along the shores of sand mixed in with the clays.

Richa was eager to learn from other artisans, their art techniques and to show them what she knew. It was as if the mind could be cleared by the sea breezes that brought new thoughts and ideas into the mind. Even the days that held sadness from losing some of her old friends did not change her ability to remain the same. There was a calm all around that could not be squelched from any out pouring of grief that came along.

Within the colony of other artists, it was like participating in a university with many teachers, eager to show the way. The sense of art was common to all those that decided to stay in such a place. It was God's own gift to bring them all together for a time and be united to find a common ground of beauty.

Richa could hardly take time out to sleep each night. There was too much to learn and too much to find. She knew that her days would be numbered as she was growing older but she would grasp every detail of life along the way. She was determined that her life would be one of meaning and was always eager to learn and to help others.

New faces appeared in the ports of Alexandria from other parts of the world on a regular basis. Richa was friends to all and a willing listener. There were many that intrigued her with their wealth of knowledge that she could glean.

She too was considered the best in her own right. She possessed wisdom that was a part of her everyday life. She never felt she had any knowledge that was not to be shared with others. Many came to her for their answers and knew that she would be kind. She shared many stories of Atlantis as she went about working with others to help them in any way that she could.

Richa designed many facets of her own art culture from the surrounding elements. Her pots of clay became known as masterpieces to many. They found her work to be quite intriguing. She told many of her visions that had given her insight to create meaningful art objects.

# EGYPT AFTER ATLANTIS

She displayed her many creative talents that she had learned on the shores of Atlantis. She again combed the beaches of Alexandria to come up with even more special pieces to melt into her own art. Clay was always a fascinating medium for her work. She used it in her art as a symbolism for showing God's ways, and that same art functioned as useful items for every day living.

Richa had a plan that she followed in the same way that she had formed a plan to follow on Atlantis. She found the challenges to be a way to seek inspiration for guiding others. It gave her an opportunity to mix with all the cultures when she helped others find shelters in this new land. Her followers were those who believed in her calling and they also helped those in need of shelters. They in turn helped others and so it was the little colony that prospered and grew in number.

It was the sea that gave Richa her first new symbol. She found stones in the shallows of the sea that glistened in the light just like she had found on the shore of Atlantis. The light penetrated through the stones and beyond as if a beacon in the water. She held these stones in her hand. They displayed a reflection much like a looking glass. She knew that creations from these stones would be looked at as miracles to show God's love.

The stones were plentiful and she found many ways to present them to others. Her followers wore them around their necks and hung them from tent poles. The stones were thought of as shields so God could protect them. Richa knew that it was not the symbol that held the meaning, but it was a way to believe in the power of God. The glow in the stone was believed to be spiritual. It was this fascination with the lights that made the stone appear to be callings from God and an enabler to hear what was coming from the soul.

Thoughts would penetrate their minds and they would believe that what they sensed were the answers that would set them free and to hear God's messages and understand the mysteries of their own soul. Richa marveled at the way they looked at her passions and were then able to believe the stones held messages from God to show them the way to their own souls for their own answers. It was a journey of the minds that made it possible to show the way to the love of God and his kind ways. It was not by the spiritual value of the stones but how the mind was able to look beyond and to know God's own messages in their own souls were for the benefit of all.

Richa and her followers set up a lighthouse on the rocks jutting out into the sea. It was not a lighthouse as you might picture in your mind now but a place in the rocks where the stones could be massed to direct the boats into the safety of the harbor.

Captains of the trade boats that came and went via the sea carried stones with them as a shield of protection from the sea. They considered them a gift from God to show them the way. They used the stones much like a compass to navigate the distance. The light from the stone reflected a certain distance and they could determine a certain marked course to navigate to another shore. It was a way to keep track of a course that they had traveled many times at sea and to know that if they followed the right course it would take them safely to their destination.

Richa made many beautiful objects from stones. Some were worn as a belief that they had a closer relationship with God. Her creations inspired many others to create their own wonders. She taught them all the art that she knew and in this way her works became part of the stories she told in sharing with others.

Some of the things that were made were for practical purposes. She used the clays of the ocean beaches and mixed them with water to form beautiful objects that she then baked to harden just as she had on Atlantis.

Her life was full and it was a good life doing God's work. She had seen Captano, Leonardo and Baylona many times over the years. Her old friends never came to the port of Alexandria without spending time with Richa. They had followed their own desire to travel down the Red Sea and on to India and beyond. Leonardo brought Richa samples of art from India that held the secrets of a new technique. She studied them closely and began to work designs into metals that she had never tried before. Baylona brought spices and shared with Richa and her friends any new ways of cooking that he had learned. Captano brought fine cloth from the Orient.

Best of all, to Richa, was the many experiences they shared that expanded her world of thinking. All that she learned from them she added to her story telling. These were happy days for all of them. Her friends never departed without taking Richa's wares and art objects with them to other ports.

The years went by and on one of their later visits it was just Leonardo and Baylona that appeared. She learned that Captano had passed on from old age. She would miss this stern, courageous man that she had learned to love like a father. Richa would never forget the kind way he had treated her as if she were his daughter. She was thankful that he had left his boat to Leonardo and she would continue to see him and Baylona as they returned to Alexandria from their trade route.

Richa was growing old and her eyesight was failing. It was more difficult each day to pursue her arts that she dearly loved. Her love for Alexandria overpowered any love she had ever found and knew she would never want to leave such a place. Egypt had been good to her. It had grown in many ways but never so great that she could not find her own place to share her stories and her art with others.

She missed her family in Italy and was saddened when she heard old age had taken her parents. She was not afraid to pass on, as she believed life would not ever be over. There would be another time and another place. It would only be this shell that would return to dust. She would take with her in her mind and soul all the memories of this life on earth. Her pattern of life would follow her. Her gifts would remain a part of her soul. God would guide her. Only her free will would give her choices.

Leonardo and Baylona were also elderly as they were near Richa's age. Richa did not realize that as her time of passing came close, Leonardo had felt a calling to depart from Italy and go directly to Alexandria without stopping at any other port. He found Richa as he had felt he would. Her eyesight was almost gone and she was growing feeble. She knew it was time to leave but she lingered long enough to bid her two friends goodbye for the last time.

Leonardo wanted to be kind and take her remains back to Italy to be with her family, but Richa refused. In her last day this is what she told him."

*"My family is mostly gone into another time as I will also go. Alexandria has become my beloved home. Where my shell lays is not important. What I leave in the hearts of others is important. My stories will be told many times by others after I am gone. I have found a colleague of sorts that has taken my thoughts and he will one day interpret them for others. I have had time to unwind by telling my stories to him and he has gladly obliged me by writing them down. I have had a wonderful life on earth and will be a part of another time very soon. I only await God's calling."*

"And so it was that God took Richa's mind and soul to another time. It seemed strange for me, being Unique now, and yet knowing I was a part of Richa's life and can sit here in the garden and tell you, my friend, of my own past life.

I have asked God many times if what I have written is correct. I have been told that it is and what I have written will be read with interest by those who have also interpreted past times. It is a story that will dwell in the minds of those who have expressed much interest in the discoveries of the past.

These stories of Atlantis will have generated new interest and one day they will fall into the hands of those who wish to search out these thoughts. I predict that it will be less than another century that those, who want to believe, will take these thoughts as written, and expose such stories as truth.

The stories will only prove that there were many different stories spread out about Atlantis. The mystery of the mind will still dwell on into future times to be rediscovered by others and to find new ways to reveal those stories. There will always be those that can find the past as revealing as I have to be interpreted for a better understanding of the present times.

I know you are asking, where did the written tablets go about Richa's life? The land itself has been covered by the sea and it has dissolved the place that the records were kept. They were placed in mass vaults during that time. It was the stories themselves that were read by scholars of the time and passed on to others. Many have challenged them but there are others who believe and one day they will find the remnants of what was once Atlantis and that will dispel all doubt that it existed.

What one must remember is that it is not the existence but what was learned from knowing the past that can benefit the present. Life is meant to be so and God allows it if we seek it."

The choices made, set the path of self-destruction.
The balance between good and evil had tilted,
and from the depths of the Earth, it was restored.

ATLANTIS *A New View*

# CHAPTER XIII:

## FROM ATLANTIS TO NOW

The first ray of light was beginning to show on the horizon. Unique had been talking literally all night. I knew that she was always determined to finish a task in a timely manner once she started, but this was different. She had already covered the major part of her story and had it on tape. I knew she must be exhausted and in need of some sleep. When I suggested that we stop for now and finish later in the day, I was surprised that she was agreeable. She must have been exhausted because when she offered tea and I refused she didn't insist.

I quickly retreated to the guestroom before she changed her mind. It had been a wonderful story and I was elated about what I had already heard. Unique's wrap up of her story would also be an interesting session, but I too was grateful to get some rest before she continued.

It was late afternoon before we made our way back to the garden. We were both refreshed after a good sleep and a delicious lunch that Unique had served.

We had hardly settled into our chairs when Unique began with what I like to refer to as her reasoning behind sharing her past with me as she continued.

**"My friend, you listened to my story of a past life. You were an attentive listener. I appreciate your undivided attention to what I had to say about my life. You may see it as only an interesting story of another time but there is much more to the true value of knowing about a past than that.**

**What I have revealed to you of a lost place called Atlantis has a real purpose. It is not the revelation of**

another time that is of value. The value is in what we can learn from a past that can help us in living our lives in the present time on earth that is important.

We both know that we are here on earth only for a very short time. We agree that when we leave this earth our shell dies and goes to dust, but our mind and soul lives on forever. Within that life form of energy we call the mind and soul, we carry with us anything we have learned from our present time as well as our past.

We believe all of this because of our faith. Believing that the passage of life passes through all time and beyond shows us how important it is to be able to draw from those memories of the soul that travels with us. We have a need to be able to refer to those experiences and to review that information like an encyclopedia.

We understand the importance of education and how the mind absorbs what we learn to use for the present and future times. Not realized by everyone, is that we also have readily available information that is held forever in our encyclopedia of our own soul. It is like a library of facts, experiences and information like no other on earth. What we find in memories is important for finding answers to questions needed for making the right choices as we continue along life's path. The most exciting revelation is that our past memories are ours to view if we choose to do so.

It is from our faith that we believe that God has given us life from our beginning. With life he allows us to experience new places for the growth of our souls. Our life on earth is one place. During our time, we can find new ways and new experiences for growth. Those are the experiences we have with us always as we are living them.

Seeking out past memories in our soul is left to us as a choice. Our past memories are our gifts to use if we choose. We are all allowed to find those memories through our belief that they are there and our desire to find them.

With this in mind, my purpose for telling you about life on Atlantis is not in discovering a place that no longer exists. My story is to give you a new awareness of how seeking out the past can bring answers that you seek for living your life in the present.

In my story you saw that the past was full of both good and evil. Where there is good there is always evil. Our present has good and evil and our future will have good and evil. What we learn about evil is how it can destroy us.

We can see that terrorism abounds on earth today and is an example of an evil that destroys. We can not control evil alone but we can bring an awareness of what happens when evil abounds. When that awareness is shared we can use our own gifts of good to fight evil in our own way. Those who choose to can find answers to their questions on how to control evil from the memories in their own souls.

You asked why God does not destroy the evil? God does not destroy what freewill and choices can control. Remember on Atlantis it was God who warned everyone through messages that Atlantis was going to fall. The warnings allowed many to choose to leave or to stay on Atlantis. Those that chose to stay were both good and evil. They made a choice with their own freewill and those who chose to stay were destroyed. In that sense their human bodies self-destructed, but they took with them to another life, experiences that would help them grow.

It is not a goal of the soul to create a physical world on earth. It is a goal of the souls to live together as one for all souls. It is not in the physical status of the body, but in the soul's creation from our beginnings, to derive a plan that will allow us to run free and help others.

We are not patterning our life to arrive on earth or another place to create that physical motion. We are a living energy to create a movement of growth. All souls are a part of the whole. Wherever the soul is placed in time it is a mass of energy for growth. That is our total goal. It is in that mass that we all survive in the universes of time. It is in that energy that we are all created to supercede any other time. In that energy of the soul we know God's love. This is the purpose of life that is recreated again and again in different body forms but still using the same energy flow of the soul through out all time.

This is reason enough to know that we must not live our lives in a way that will only benefit ourselves. The plan set out for us in the beginning by a higher power is to live with peace and kindness. This is the good that God intended us to find. Always evil exists. Where there is good there is evil, but good must prevail for the growth of the soul.

If we cast our minds off into a direction that good will never surface, we have lost the ability to penetrate into a growth that is obtained with love and kindness. Good is a way of igniting the growth of the soul for a positive energy force and thus creating a greater life.

Life on earth is a release from another home that allows the mind and soul to be a part of another plan and to rebuild. It is a way to be a part of a bigger plan for all.

By becoming a part of this world on earth we have our own agenda that will surface through our freewill and desires. When it is our time to move on it will resurface in other times, again and again. We are a part of life on earth with a plan that equates to better ways of seeing the way God intended us to see.

Being on earth we regroup and that allows us to know there is a bigger plan to bring all souls together through out time. It is a way that we are all working together to formulate a better way to see.

Think of this, if earth was chosen for you to find a place to develop the mind, then you would want to revisit any past information that you carry in the memory of your mind and soul. This would allow you to assert any thoughts that could assist you in seeing better ways for your growth as well as the growth of other souls.

It is in that stimulus that the mind is open to thoughts that can be a positive plan for the good of all. Earth is a place that we can find those memories from our mind and soul and add new thoughts that may have been lost. It allows the soul a refresher course. In this manner we learn that the possession of knowledge from other times is not harmful to our souls but allows the mind a clearer path that will forever resurface in all times.

The evil that raises its ugly head in our world on earth is present with the good. The evil is brought on by choices from mankind for the purpose of control and greed. Evil will not be allowed to take over completely as long as good exists. God does not destroy. Evil self - destructs from the choices made.

ATLANTIS *A New View*

It was a sign of the times that Atlantis unfolded in a quest to dissolve a past and create a present for others. It is not a history that should be repeated but a history that should be known so that no one else will dwell on those ways and no one else will have to go through those degrees. Evil would not have destroyed had they changed their ways to live life for the good.

Let us visit the past of three people that once lived on Atlantis as I did. Those same souls exist here on earth today and have their own stories from the past. From these stories you will see how knowing the past is of real value in finding answers to our present lives in different ways.

Mohamed was his name from long ago. Today he is known as Charles. Our story begins with Mohamed on Atlantis where he was a doctor. He had heard of the experiments and wanted to achieve his own glory in what they were able to accomplish. He was a man that had learned how skin could be transplanted onto another human and become a new growth. What he was doing had merit but he wanted more than grafting skin. He wanted to research all ways to find the fountain of youth.

He went to Atlantis with exuberance to pass on his own beliefs and to see clearly how he could accomplish more. He was welcomed into the experimental arena that he discovered there. He believed it was a way to advance his own skills.

What Mohamed did not realize was the greed and evil that lived here. He became a part of the evil process that was butchering man against their will by leading them into believing they would receive in return, strength like no other man.

# FROM ATLANTIS TO NOW

Mohamed soon learned this sequence of butchery developed monsters and he began to plot in his own way to save as many as he could from this terrible wrong. He would take as many as he could under the guise of his own experiments and tell the authorities that his subjects had died. Actually he had released them to return to their own homes to gather their families and quickly leave the island before they could be caught again.

Mohammed had within himself the desire to do good and when he found that his own plan of glorifying his knowledge meant destroying others, it was more than he could fathom. He stayed on Atlantis as long as he thought it was safe to help others but in time he was found out. Before the evil ones could avenge him, the tremors were more frequent and it was easy to take refuge on one of the boats that was ready to go.

He was never caught and took with him the knowledge that medicine should stay in control for the good of mankind. He went to another place far away and explored other avenues. With his knowledge and his mind, he developed new medicines that helped others grow old. He turned to herbs that he had found on Atlantis that could easily have the potions that readily developed the minds for well being.

That was his past and today he again lives on earth. He is called Charles and lives in Maine by the sea. He is not a doctor, but develops the land in ways that the soil is enriched, so that it can grow healthy crops that are to be harvested. He is an environmentalist of sorts and believes that what is taken from the land must go back to build the soil and make it richer. He is what you would call a horticulturist of today. His past life has allowed him to learn, in many ways.

# ATLANTIS *A New View*

We move on to the life of Samuel as he was known on Atlantis. Samuel was a man that was not pleasant to know. He was hand picked as a bodyguard of the king and a guard of the palace. He was a man who liked to be in control. He had no care for others and held the villagers at his own mercy. Samuel only cared that he had the power to take innocent men that were careless, and use them as experiments for the evil. When the process did not work, he willingly cast them into the ocean below.

He did not keep track of how many perished at his own hands but he was marked with a past that would relate to those slayings. Samuel was brutal and nasty to all those that came his way and he did not agree that they should have rights of their own. He did not care for life in any way, except for the desire to bring himself gold.

He used brut force and went along with the evil, right up to the end of the fall of Atlantis. He perished with all of the rest when the island was engulfed into the ocean on that fateful day.

Today he is still learning from his own past decay from long ago. What he did in his past had to be corrected in his future. It has taken him great lengths to turn his disarray into a positive link with life. He does not kill today. He helps those that have been savagely beaten by others. He has learned that brut force does not mix with those that wish to live in a peaceful way. He is now sharing a life with those that help others in crisis situations when they have been exposed to the wrong elements. He is a social worker. He lives in a forest that is always green. The route he takes to work through this greenery brings him a sense of peace. He knows that he has helped those that have been exposed to harsh ways.

# FROM ATLANTIS TO NOW

He lives in Colorado, in a small town, that is exposed to lots of traffic. He finds many in his small town that need help in finding their own freedoms.

His name is Benjamin but he goes by Jed. He is strong in his actions and is quick to delay fights and helps shelter those that need to be protected.

He has turned his life around from his past on Atlantis. He senses that what happened to him in the past must not be repeated again. He realizes that the growth of the soul comes from the good one can do for others and he is spending this lifetime on a course of good. What he has developed from his past has given him the courage to make a difference in this life.

Last but not least is another story of a life on Atlantis. He was Gabriel in that time and now on earth is a lady called Sarah. She has made great strides in changing her ways from the time spent on Atlantis.

Gabriel of Atlantis was a man who believed himself to be a statesman of sorts. In those times a statesman was an overseer of subjects that could be manipulated. He arrived on Atlantis to persuade others to work for him in the many plants of the evil ones and to carry on their tasks of changing men.

Those that worked in those buildings of evil were feared by those all around. They were treated like royalty from the king. They would find subjects that could be changed forever in their own appearances.

Gabriel led them on the searches in the villages to find the next victims for the experiments. He above all was feared because of his own ruthless mind. He had little passion for others. He stayed on the island to help the evil ones until the end. He died because he could not see that life was not to be controlled by others.

His soul had been led astray by those promises of riches. His soul possessed a pattern that could be led astray by a passion that would only give him the gold. His soul was tainted and his time of redemption was faced in another time and another degree by a higher power.

It is Sarah of today that has lived in complete control but has learned that her own control must not control others. She has lived lives of bondage after Atlantis and has found the other side. She has learned the importance of controlling ones own will and knows that she has been blessed with the choices of finding the right times.

Sarah has achieved today her own wealth of knowledge by leading others into an arena that allows them to control their own wills. She is blessed with the looks to impress many but also a will to give her knowledge to other minds so they can see the best of all. She acknowledges that the wealth of knowledge, by her own claim, is to find the best work of art. She persuades many to create their own art form and circulates many works of art into museums.

She does not live in the U.S. but is of a European culture that persuades others to find their gifts to create more wonders that she can share. It is our own justice that allows us to make our own time right and still help others. That is what gives us the control to find the knowledge of our own souls. It is in that wonder that more love is created and the energy becomes positive so that the negative forces are oppressed.

The soul and mind are the energy forces that hold a past we can reach into to view and to use for answers that can benefit us in the present times. It is in our own beliefs and desires that we find those energy forces.

If I had but one lesson to leave you it would not be in knowing about Atlantis. It would be about understanding how the evil that resided there among the good, set a path for self-destruction, just by the choices made.

Good and evil are like hot and cold. You can not know of the cold without the hot, or the hot without the cold. You know that you need both. It is in that balance that we seek our past to find the good, and then share that positive enlightenment, so all can prosper.

Destroying evil with force is the message that circulates the most today. It is not in the destroying, but in the choices of good over evil, that develops our minds into peacefulness, and that can radiate the energy of love. In this way, it allows each of us to grow, and the universe to expand, which creates growth for all. This is not a story of the fall of Atlantis, but a story of the rise of human kind, for the love that God has allowed us to find."

I sat in awe as Unique spoke the last sentence. It was a story that lives on for me in knowing that human kind passes with it those desires to make it right for all. Our gifts, along with God's own love, turns the past destructions into new life, to be seeded by all who believe in his power to live and love forever.

## WARNING

**Atlantis represented a creation of man empowered with evil deeds.**
**It destroyed what God had given freely, to meet all of man's needs.**
**Atlantis is God's warning to never repeat a time of destroying, out of complete greed.**

**ORDER FORM:**
## ATLANTIS *A NEW VIEW*
### AUTHOR: LOUISE INGRAHAM
**PUBLISHED BY:**
**BIZY ENTERPRISES, INC.**
**929 N. VAL VISTA DRIVE**
**SUITE 107 #191**
**GILBERT, AZ. 85234**

WEB ORDERING: WWW. MINDSEYEVISION.COM
OR
MAIL ORDER:

Each Book $21.95: Quanity:_____ Total $_____
Shipping & Handling:
U.S. $4.95 for first book---------------------$_____
$2.95 for each additional book------------ $_____
7.8% Sales Tax for Arizona addresses---$_____
    SUB TOTAL                            $_____
International shipping:
$10.00 first book
$5.00 each additional book
    TOTAL AMOUNT:--------------------- $_____
        ENCLOSE CHECK OR MONEY ORDER

MAIL TO:
NAME:_____
STREET:_____
CITY:_____STATE_____
ZIP:_____
E-MAIL: _____
SEE WEB SITE FOR OTHER BOOK OFFERINGS:
WWW. MINDSEYEVISION.COM

ATLANTIS *A New View*

www.ingramcontent.com/pod-product-compliance
Lightning Source LLC
Chambersburg PA
CBHW020759160426
43192CB00006B/377